LESSONS FROM THE

BUSINESS

HEROES

OF THE PANDEMIC

Duane McHodgkins

Lessons from the Business Heroes of the Pandemic
Published by DM Positive Publishing
Parker, Colorado

ISBN: 978-1-7369579-0-5
BUSINESS & ECONOMICS / Personal Success

Cover and Interior design by Victoria Wolf, wolfdesignandmarketing.com

To Anneeda

Thanks for supporting my book!

Stay Essential!

[signature]

To my wife and children, thank you for the support
and encouragement during this process. Your positive
attitudes made it possible for me to complete it.

CONTENTS

LIST OF CONTRIBUTORS

AFTER EXHAUSTING all the information and ideas I had for this book, I decided to interview a number of people who I consider Business Heroes of the Pandemic. I wanted to see what others did and what they saw during these difficult times. They come from a number of different industries, and each of them handled this time in different ways. Their stories were very motivating. They are all very busy people, so I had to get creative in finding time to interview them.

I am listing their names and occupations here, and I will refer to them by first name throughout the book when I talk about their individual stories. In the true spirit of the year, I interviewed most of them using Zoom, not necessarily for social distancing purposes, but so I could record the sessions and not have to take notes (not one of my strongest skills, so I found a better way). A couple of them were so busy that we just exchanged emails back and forth over a number of days instead. Since all these people had such great stories, I didn't want to miss anything they said. That is probably one good thing about the pandemic time; it has forced us all to find new, different, and better ways to do things, such as using Zoom. (See Rule Number 7). This book is filled with many more ways to do things differently or better.

I am very thankful for these people, and I could not have completed this project without their insights and willingness to share their ideas and experiences. Thank you, Business Heroes!

- **Benjamin "BK" Martin** – Mortgage Loan Officer with Alliance Mortgage Group

- **Gary Goldwasser** – Business Broker with TransWorld Business Advisors

- **Monika Anderson** – Owner of Kameleon Digital Marketing

- **John Bocker** – CEO/Cofounder, FFL Consultants, consultants to the firearms industry

- **Suzanne Hogan** – Realtor with Worth Clark Realty

- **Charity Phillips** – Personal Chef

- **Nina Anderson** – Executive Director, WineShop at Home

- **Alicia Soto** – Owner, ETO Inc. Insurance

- **Marisa Huston** – Podcaster, Live Blissed Out

- **Miranda Lopez** – Backpack journalist for a midmarket television station

- **Lynn Hurlburt** – Owner/Stylist, Parker Hair Xpress

In addition to these people, I am also including many stories from conversations I have had with others over the many months I spent writing this book.

INTRODUCTION

THE EVENTS OF 2020 and 2021 have affected everyone in major ways. Many people found themselves unemployed
or with their hours drastically cut. Many business owners could
not keep things going and were forced to close or sell for a loss.
The number of people getting behind in their mortgages or rent
payments has skyrocketed. Many people are genuinely hurting
financially and emotionally.

As I have watched the events unfold, I was saddened by the
businesses that had to shut their doors, never to return, and the
individuals who lost their source of income and didn't know
where to turn for help. I have watched as longer and longer
lines have appeared at food pantries. After spending a couple of
months feeling helpless about these businesses and individuals,
I came up with the idea for this book.

I don't want to minimize those who did all they could
by putting in long hours and struggling to keep their heads
above water and still could not make their businesses survive,

but I noticed a group of people I call the Business Heroes of the Pandemic. They didn't accept the way things were. They decided to think outside the box. They didn't "stay in their lane" or "color inside the lines." They stepped up and kept their worlds from crumbling. They kept their doors open. They kept their families fed and their employees working. This book is filled with examples of how they responded to the challenges, and I think we can all learn how to do the same things regardless of the situation we find ourselves in. The biggest lesson here is **don't wait until something happens to you—work on these things now** (see Rule Number 9) so the next time something like this happens, you can be better prepared.

Shortly after the government decided to close all businesses deemed "nonessential," there were many who listened to the government officials who said, "We need two weeks to flatten the curve," and simply hoped it would all be over soon and the financial damage they encountered would be fairly small. I call this the Ostrich Model. They put their heads in the sand and took on a sort of victim mentality and decided there was nothing they could do about it. Here we are several months later, and many businesses are still shut down or running at less than 50 percent capacity. Even businesses and individuals who are extremely strong financially can't survive at the 50 percent or less level for very long.

More than anything else, this caused the feeling of a loss of control for many people. Some handled it by fighting back and protesting and some by giving up. But there were others who did more than just hope for better times or complain; they chose to find a new way to survive. Watching these people has inspired me to make changes and improvements in my business and my personal life, to help me avoid being deemed "nonessential" in the future. Nothing is foolproof, but if you take these ideas to heart and apply them to your own life, regardless of whether you own a business or work for a company, you can ensure you will always be "essential."

I used many examples from the restaurant industry for this book because restaurants were hit extremely hard, and they were much more visible than other industries. In my area, it is hard to drive down a major street and not see examples of successful restaurants and some that didn't find a way to survive. This includes my favorite restaurant. I am saddened every time I drive by and see the building boarded up. I remember the last time I went there was just before the government closed down all restaurants. I had gone there with my family to celebrate my birthday.

I mention a number of my favorite books in this writing. They helped me come up with some of these ideas and might be good resources as you research and try to expand on some of the ideas presented here. I also include many quotes that have kept me going during difficult times, and I hope they will do the same for you.

Below are some of the characteristics I have seen in the Business Heroes of the Pandemic, and in the following chapters I explain the rules they taught me. I have included as many examples as I could in order to give you more ideas. The purpose of this book is not to go in depth and explain exactly how to do the things I list. There are already plenty of other books that do that. No, the purpose of this book is to give you some ideas you can research yourself and use to move forward. (See Rule Number 9.) This is the sample course; you need to use it to find some ideas that make sense to you and make them your own.

Some of the stories have different rules that overlap, and I list the other rules for reference when that happens. Following these rules in conjunction with other rules will enhance your results.

All this advice isn't for everyone. Each of our situations is different, but you can pull out at least an idea or two from this book and use them to improve your own situation, so the next time a worldwide pandemic or a personal tragedy happens, you will be better prepared. As Epictetus, the Greek stoic philosopher said, "It's not what happens to you, but how you react to it that matters."

Characteristics of Business Heroes of the Pandemic

I have complied a list of the characteristics that helped these Business Heroes remain successful even in the most difficult times.

- Business Heroes realize there is no perfect time to start something new, so they make the most of today instead of waiting for the best time or the right time.

- Business Heroes don't beat themselves up if they make a mistake. They learn from it and move forward anyway.

- Business Heroes know that everything is subject to change, so they don't count on any one thing to see them through.

- Business Heroes diversify. They know there are times when certain markets are going up and other markets might be flat or shrinking.

- Business Heroes know that "this too shall pass." They choose to hold on and keep moving forward.

- Business Heroes travel in packs. They understand that always being the "lone wolf" leaves you vulnerable. They seek wise counsel.

- Business Heroes travel in the right packs. They stay away from those who try to bring them down. They avoid "crab mentality" when those who try to improve themselves are pulled back by the group, just like crabs that are trying to escape a pot are pulled back in by the other crabs.

- Business Heroes stay active. They know that choosing to do nothing is still making a choice and that is not the choice you want to make.

- Business Heroes keep a positive attitude. They understand that whether you think you can or you think you can't, you are right.

- Business Heroes don't settle for mediocre. They expect the best from themselves and for themselves.

- Business Heroes communicate: to their customers, to their suppliers, to their employees.

- Business Heroes know that tomorrow is a new day. They don't dwell on the past. They learn from it and move on.

- Business Heroes plan ahead so they can stay prepared.

- Business Heroes are persistent and consistent.

I encourage you to keep a pen and paper handy and take notes as you read through the stories and get ideas. That way, you can take full advantage of your ideas and not forget them. On my website, www.BusinessHeroesOfThePandemic.com, I will list more resources that you can use to dig deeper into the ideas presented here.

After each rule, I have included a brief recap of the major ideas from that chapter, and there are a few questions to help you get started with the ideas from this book. I encourage you to take some time and think about these and either fill in your answers on the book or on a separate paper (see Rule Number 9) in case you plan to pass this book along to someone else.

RULE NUMBER 1

Always be looking for ways to reinvent yourself or your business— the Back to the Drawing Board Model

EVEN IN THE BEST OF TIMES, you need to look ahead to ensure circumstances aren't moving in a different direction than you are moving. You should always evaluate what is working and what isn't working through the lens of the current climate (financial, political, and weather).

Many years ago, Netflix initially started as a DVD rental mail delivery service. Its major competition was Blockbuster, Hollywood Video, Redbox, and other similar businesses. Customers had to go to the Netflix website, browse for titles they wanted, wait three days for the DVDs to arrive in their mailbox, and then mail them back when they had finished watching them so they could order more. Netflix realized the mail delivery model was not sustainable and switched to mostly streaming movies and shows, and it has been phenomenally successful while most of its competitors during the DVD days have disappeared. I still see Redbox kiosks occasionally, but the rest are gone. Actually, Netflix still rents DVDs through the mail. Some people like this option because their list to rent is vast, and others like it because they live in rural areas where high-speed internet isn't available yet. Netflix didn't quit the rent-by-mail business; it just found another way that was more profitable and popular. So, just like Kleenex brand became the catchall term for tissue, Google for search engines, and Jell-O for gelatin, Netflix is now a universal term for the entire industry.

Is the status quo sustainable?

During the initial shutdown of businesses, many restaurants were forced to close immediately. Here are a few ways that successful restauranteurs weathered this storm.

I know of a few restaurants that had planned to remodel in the future and took this time to complete the remodel, since they were already closed. (See Rule Number 2.) Some even used their employees to handle as much as they could by having them do the cleaning or painting at a distance from each other to meet the government recommendations. This was a great way to keep their employees busy working even when the business was closed. I am sure these employees appreciated the stability of being able to continue working.

There were restaurants that moved to a grocery store model to get rid of all their perishable foods so they could avoid taking a loss. They had to act fast, since all these items had a short shelf life. They had to pay for all that inventory, so just waiting was not an option. Their creditors wouldn't wait, and if the food spoiled, they could not have sold it. I remember a large frozen box truck sitting in the steakhouse parking lot in my town. The restaurant was selling a complete meal that customers could take home and cook. It even included the cooking instructions.

There were restaurants that quickly converted to a pickup or delivery service, and some even used their servers as delivery drivers or signed on with delivery services to keep the doors open. Some of them shortened their menus to make the transition more manageable for their staff. According to Marketwatch.com, "The pandemic has more than doubled food-delivery apps' business."

Many printing shops recognized this trend and heavily marketed the fact that they make large signs and banners for storefronts. At the same time, the delivery services were trying to pump up their ranks to meet this new demand.

Many website developers switched from whatever they were doing to creating new websites or improving existing websites for restaurants. They knew this was a great opportunity that wouldn't last. Some even put other jobs on hold since those customers' companies were not currently open.

I know many people who lost their jobs or had their hours drastically cut, so they answered the call from these delivery services to supplement their income. Many others applied to work in grocery stores, since those stores were considered essential and needed more help because everyone was shopping more and even hoarding supplies.

As the regulations slowly lifted, many restaurants converted their sidewalks for outside dining to increase the number of diners they were allowed to serve. Fast-food restaurants converted to a drive-through-only model, meaning they did not have to constantly sanitize their dining rooms, which saved them time and money. As the closures moved into the fall and it became too cold outside for patio dining, many restaurants added enclosures to keep patrons warm and socially distanced from each other. Even national chains that don't normally have patios got into the trend. I have seen signs at the International House of Pancakes (IHOP) offering patio dining. Who would have ever thought this would be an option anyone would want? People probably have gone to IHOP and sat in its "patio" just so they can say they did it.

Rule Number 1

I know of a restaurant that purchased thirty ice fishing tents and added heaters in them on its patio and part of its parking lot. These tents seat eight, so they could even handle larger groups. The restaurant has had many customers post pictures of these on social media, and that will further increase sales. The last post I saw about the restaurant said it now has fifty tents. The owners definitely found a way to reinvent the restaurant and, in the process, got a lot of people talking about it. I have many friends who went to eat there just to see all the tents. This is more than just surviving; this is thriving! I tried to stop there for lunch recently, and since I didn't have a reservation, my wait would have been more than an hour and a half. I opted to go somewhere else and try again when I am better prepared and have a reservation.

In downtown Denver, a group of restaurants got together and convinced the city to close down a side street, which they all used for outside dining. Customers simply had to check in at the restaurant of their choice and go to a table, and that restaurant's servers would come and take their orders and serve them outside in the street.

Other industries found ways to reinvent themselves as well. Consultants and therapists embraced the camera and converted their practices to video meetings. This has changed the entire industry, and most say they will remain virtual even after restrictions are removed. One therapist I spoke with said many of her patients feel more comfortable meeting virtually because they are in their own space. This also means therapists are not stuck with getting new clients only in their immediate vicinity. They are free to pursue clients almost anywhere, depending on any license or certification that might be required. They are also saving money by not having to rent an office or drive to that office. (See Rule Number 8.)

I have talked to therapists who are considering moving to a smaller town or a warmer climate since they don't have to physically live where their practice is located any more. In his book, *The 4-Hour Workweek*, Tim Ferriss talks a lot about how to convince your boss to let you work from home. Now, with the pandemic, most office personnel are required to work from home.

Construction and remodel companies were offering discounts to get people to do their home improvements now rather than later. This allowed the companies to keep their employees working and not on unemployment. They knew if they laid off their workers many of them would never come back. My wife and I took advantage of this and got our kitchen remodeled for about 20 percent less than if we had waited.

Even in the public sector, there are examples of organizations remaking themselves to better handle the current times. Most public libraries set up a system that allowed their members to choose books online and pick them up at their local branch. A library staff member would deliver the books to the trunk of the member's car so they remained touch-free. Other government agencies switched to appointments only to keep from having an office full of people.

Retail stores and grocery stores used a similar process, allowing customers to purchase online, pull up in the parking lot, and call the store, prompting an employee to bring out their purchases and place them in the customer's vehicle. This allowed the stores to stay open and the customers to continue to get their needed products.

Miranda, the reporter listed earlier as a contributor, interviewed a couple of retailers that decided to move their entire inventory online so they could still help customers who couldn't physically come into their stores. A running shoe store gave its customers the option to get their purchases shipped or they could do curbside pickup. During the Christmas season, the store had this option available for Small Business Saturday, and over that weekend it received fifty-five shipping orders. The store was able to change and adapt to keep its customers and stay in business.

Zoos around the world have faced the loss of revenue since closing down. Their revenue is used to feed the animals, keep up the facilities, and pay the staff. There were even reports that some zoos might have to slaughter some animals to feed others, although I have not found any evidence that this actually happened. Due to this challenge, many zoos have gone online to showcase their animals and show behind-the-scenes activities to try to build viewership. They even conducted virtual fundraising and offered online subscriptions. Zoos are streaming feedings and care of babies, holding naming contests for those babies, creating virtual tours on their YouTube channels, or doing Facebook Live. Many zoos also now have Instagram channels and post many times daily to increase online traffic and hopefully gain more necessary funding.

Is there something new I can add to my mix?

If you own a business, is there a product or service that complements your current offerings? Adding something new is a great way to become more needed by your current customers or gain an opportunity to acquire new customers. If you sell paint, you should add paint brushes and other painting supplies. If you mow lawns, you should also apply weed-and-feed and maybe even prune bushes and trees. These are very simple ideas, and I am sure most, if not all, paint sellers also sell paint brushes, but you get the general idea. Find those complementary items to add to your mix. Imagine if you could increase your average sale by 10, 15, or even 20 percent on a consistent basis. I did this a few years ago when I started selling antivirus products since a lot of my work is cleaning up virus-infected computers and many people didn't have adequate antivirus protection. (See Rule Number 4.)

I know a doctor who minored in marketing while in college and had been very successful with his own marketing and search engine optimization (SEO), so he decided to start a side business online offering marketing help for other small businesses. He had the expertise, and since his practice was closed, he spent that time creating something new. (See Rule Number 2.)

When masks were recommended or required, there were many screen-printing businesses that converted their screen-printing to masks instead of T-shirts. They didn't wait for their business to dry up; they added to the mix. When this is over, masks might become permanent fixtures for some people, and these businesses have effectively increased their product lineup. Searching on Google, I found many that will print just about anything on masks, in addition to all the creations they have come up with, and some will even match a customer's outfit. I've seen convenience stores, hair salons, and dry cleaners that had homemade masks for sale. I've even seen a few people on street corners selling cloth masks. On Etsy, there are also numerous people selling custom handmade masks. Many major companies are providing their employees with masks that have the company logo on them. Some enterprising companies or individuals sold them on that idea.

Once the malls were allowed to open up again, my son went to our local mall and found a store called Covid-19 Essentials. I am sure this store won't be around for long after this pandemic is over, but in the meantime, whoever created this store will probably make a decent living selling these supplies. (See Rule Number 7.)

Were you aware that Chuck E. Cheese Pizza was selling premium pizza and wings on DoorDash under the name Pasqually's Pizza & Wings? (Pasqually is one of the characters in the chain's mechanical band.) No one would ever request the basic pizza available at Chuck E. Cheese for delivery when there are so many much-better-tasting alternatives. Faced with not having opportunities to serve in its dining rooms, with all the mechanical characters and video games to draw a crowd, Chuck E. Cheese decided to improve the quality and taste of its product and sell to consumers who wanted delivery. I don't know if this business will survive, but at least the chain is not just giving up. It's doing something. (See Rule Number 9.)

A great way to add to the mix is to give something away. Usually, this means information. Both Gary, the business broker, and Monika, the digital marketing expert, mentioned this as something they did. Monika told me, "I did some promotions and giveaways. The freebies I offered were advice that people needed, and later some felt like investing in my services based on that. Mostly website help. I gave away a free in-depth website consultation. It was about a $200 value and came with pages of notes to improve their sites. Some of the people who received this said they thought the same things about their sites and were glad for the confirmation, and they went ahead and took care of it themselves, while a few asked me to completely redesign their sites."

Gary said, "I first started off as being a resource. What can I give? How can I help? Providing information as soon as it was available for small businesses on loans and other support. Supporting small businesses. I was persistent and consistent."

John, the firearms consultant, told me, "I was very fortunate. The firearms industry thrived for the first six or seven months, and just now we are starting to feel the effects of a lack of supply chain. As a consultant in this industry, I keep my customers out of trouble with the ATF. I am like the CPA who comes in and cleans up your books before the IRS shows up for an audit. I spent much of my career in risk management and even worked on pandemic preparedness at companies for the past twenty years. Even with all this, no one had ever lived through a pandemic like this. At the beginning, I knew it would last more than ninety days. I knew it was going to be bad. I was perfectly placed to become a self-appointed expert on this topic, and I already had a history with the firearms trade association as being a communicator, a blogger at their conventions, and ended up as their consultant for crisis pandemic preparedness and kept their customers up to date. I also started a newsletter to all of my customers to help them navigate this."

John realized that travel, which was a large part of what he did, was going to end for quite a while. He was traveling to gun shops and working with them in person and realized he needed another way to make money when travel shut down. "So, I started this newsletter to become the go-to guy in the industry. The trade association is paying me to stay home and answer questions for their members. So, I have created this huge audience, and I keep them informed as to what is going on in the industry due to the pandemic. I have also increased the subscriptions for my company. [See Rule Number 4.] The industry came to a halt, and I just jumped in the middle of it and started talking about it. It has made me the expert and increased my company's profits and helped our marketing. "

Charity, the personal chef, did a lot of adding to the mix: "Before the pandemic, I was working out of people's houses and doing events. When the pandemic hit, pretty much all of my customers stopped hiring me, so I found a commercial kitchen and started cooking there and then started delivering to my personal chef customers. But they still weren't coming back fast enough. So, we came up with this Saturday night meal delivery. We did that for a little while, and I redid my website so I could take orders. It was kind of a quick fix, just throwing something at the wall. In May, when the restaurants started reopening, we stopped getting our business for the

Saturday night meal delivery. We quit that in June and went back to doing personal chef customers and that wasn't enough business, so I started totally redoing my website in the middle of the summer using Shopify. We ended up having to switch kitchens again because the owner was being unreasonable. September was my worst month of the year because of moving and everything else. I launched my new website the beginning of October, and I totally changed my marketing. We went back to meal delivery, but we do it on Wednesday nights and we also do retreats and personal chef work too. So, between the three of those, we have been really busy and also started selling these homemade chocolates. We have thrown everything at the wall pretty much."

When asked if there was anything she would have told herself in the beginning, knowing what she knows now, she said: "I think I would tell myself not to panic, realize that I have the ability to figure out new things to do, and just keep trying. Because you will find something that works if you just keep trying. It is just a matter of not giving up." She kept pivoting to find the right mix. This also fits in with Rule Number 9.

Nina had to reinvent her business. "I am a rep for a Napa winery. It is a direct sales business; it is like Mary Kay for wine. I have been with them for twelve years. We teach people in a fun and casual way about wine. We mainly do this through in-home wine tastings with six to twelve friends. With the shutdown, we can't do any in-home tastings.

"For the first couple of months, it did shut me down completely, because I couldn't do in-home tastings, because I had been trained for eleven and a half years to do my business model this way. So I had to take a stop and a step back. So initially, what I did was serviced my existing customers, kept their stock filled, reaching out to them with new specials and promotions and keeping that in the forefront. Then we started doing virtual wine tastings. So that was a new skill that I had to develop, and I had to teach it to my team as well. We went from meeting people in person and now we are jumping on a Zoom call and doing virtual tastings. And I have to be honest—in the beginning it was a little awkward. It was like you and I are just sitting here talking about wine and I get to my closing and say, 'So this is how you can order wine.' And it was this awkward moment when I don't have a room where we can go into away from the group where you and I can talk about your order. Instead, everybody is sitting there together. So, the thought was, *I guess I will follow up with everybody after the Zoom call.* I went from getting immediate orders to almost taking a week to get all the orders from one tasting.

"The follow-up became very cumbersome. We had to take that and think, *How can we massage this to make it more streamlined like we do with in-person tastings?* So, we started getting the contact information from everyone up front, so we had an easier way to get in touch with them at the end of the tasting. Then, we figured out we could use the breakout rooms in Zoom to privately get their orders while everyone else was still talking in the main room. We also had the host move their laptop into another room for us to talk to individuals who were meeting with the host in-person so we could get their orders.

We figured out how to get the orders during the event instead of having to try to contact them afterwards."

I saw a funny picture recently on social media that said, "The fact that Hooters hasn't launched a home delivery service called Knockers just seems like a missed business opportunity to me!" Yes, this is funny, but it also shows that you never know what you can create to remake your business. Many great ideas start out as just a joke and then someone says, "Why not?"

Rule Number 1 Recap

In this chapter, we talked about how things will change, and that you need to stay relevant. We all want to be like Netflix and survive and become the universal term for our industries. We talked about restaurants that figured out how to survive by going back to the drawing board. We talked about other businesses that also found that their status quo wasn't right, so they changed.

We looked at businesses and individuals who didn't take no for an answer and found a way to stay in business. Based on the examples, it appears that almost anyone can find a way to reinvent themselves if they try.

We also talked about adding something to the mix. If you sell paint, you should sell paint brushes also. If your main business is not working right now, how can you change it? Look at Chuck E. Cheese Pizza, or Pasqually's Pizza & Wings.

Some of my contributors discussed ways they were able to add to the mix: give away information, become the expert, keep pivoting and don't give up, keep making changes and improvements.

DO THE WORK

How have you already used this rule in your life?

Can you add anything to this?

What idea(s) from this rule can you implement in your life?

1.

2.

3.

List your action steps to do this:

1.

2.

3.

RULE NUMBER 2

Use the current time to grow— the Butterfly Model

THE WHOLE IDEA for the Butterfly Model came from the fact that there were so many people stuck at home, not working, not shopping, and not visiting friends or extended family. Many people were just spending their time binge-watching shows, staying up way too late, and sleeping away the day. When you go through a time when you can't currently move forward and feel stuck or feel like you have no control, the best thing you can do is prepare and plan to move forward in the future. Doing that will give you back some of the control over your life.

Take the current time to work on yourself and improve yourself, much like the caterpillar does inside the cocoon. What looks like the end of life to a casual observer is actually a brand-new beginning—a metamorphosis that enables this former caterpillar who was only able to crawl along the ground or on a leaf in a tree to be able to reach new heights and fly as a beautiful new creature. We can do the same thing.

Many companies were not allowed to open their doors, but they were able to work from home and keep their businesses moving forward. I know of some insurance agents who were not adversely affected financially by the pandemic, but still used the time to increase their position in the community. They had face shields made with their company name and logo on the band, and they donated these to hospitals, no strings attached (and no pun intended). But this goodwill gesture might pay off in the future when those doctors or nurses need new renters, homeowners, or auto insurance policies.

There were people who went back to school online to complete certifications or degrees since they had the extra time. Time will pass either way, so why not come out the other side with new or improved skills? Even after the pandemic is over, there will be opportunities for online schooling that can be accomplished on the weekends or during your off hours. Some are even self-paced. Again, time will pass whether you do something or not. If you mainly just want to learn new skills, and you don't necessarily need that "piece of paper" (degree, diploma, certification), you could just get some books or even watch YouTube videos and learn from those instead of spending a lot of money on classes. (See Rule Number 8.)

If you find your business is being sidelined by forces beyond your control, you can use the extra time you have available to redo your website, rewrite your operations manual, remodel your company, improve your SEO (search engine optimization), learn or improve a skill, or create a mailing list or phone number list or email list of your customers so you can communicate with them. (See Rule Number 6.) Use your cocoon time to move yourself and your business forward. In his book, *The E-Myth Revisited*, Michael Gerber talks about the fact that over 80 percent of small businesses fail. This is partly due to the fact that business owners have not set up their businesses for success by having easy-to-replicate systems in place. If this sounds like your business, take this downtime to write out and refine your processes so you can have a system to help you grow again when that is possible. Who knows? This might make it possible for you to franchise your business in the future.

I just read an article about a resort hotel in Hawaii that had been preparing for a $15 million renovation and had just started it in January 2020. The plans called for at least an eighteen-month timeline, with many interruptions to the workings in the hotel. After the hotel was forced to shut down in March 2020, the owners were able to accelerate the timeline to only twelve months. That means their guests will be less impacted and probably enjoy their visits more, and the owners will see more profit, since they finished up early and won't have to run at less than full capacity for another six months.

Lynn, the salon owner, did the same thing. "It was actually very good timing for me. I got to remodel my salon in April since It was closed. I felt the pandemic starting in January, and my restart for my business was set for February. I started my website but didn't really do anything else to get my business going."

Driving through downtown Denver during the pandemic, I saw road construction and detours everywhere. It wasn't a problem since traffic was so light. So, it was pretty obvious that the city was also taking advantage of the light traffic to speed up those projects. This probably saved the city (or at least the construction company) some money and saved many drivers time and headaches when things opened up again.

I know a young man who wanted to become a personal trainer, but since all gyms were closed, he could not find employment similar to his goals. In fact, he did get hired a couple times by gyms, but before he could start, he was told there had been a freeze on hiring so he couldn't start work. He looked online and found that the major certifications for personal trainers could be taken completely on his computer. During the lockdown time, he took the required courses and came through it with new career opportunities.

Monika decided to take some online classes. "I feel like a lot of us have gained some time since we don't have to drive to meet people or maybe we lost a little business and have more time from that. I have gained about five to eight hours a week. I have used that time to sign up for classes online for self-development. I took a coaching program, and I signed up for a book club, a class on world literature, and a basic conscientiousness class. Every two months, I sign up for a new class."

Suzanne, the realtor, had this to say about the initial shutdown and how she handled it: "It slowed down the rentals; it didn't at first, because I had a lot in my pipeline. What it really caused me to do was switch companies. I was thinking about it, but since I was doing okay with rentals, I didn't need to work on the sales part of real estate. But when the rentals slowed down, and they were taking half of my commission on the sales, I had to make a change."

She also took the time to improve her situation. She found a project where she could take part in writing a book. "Technically, I did not write the whole book. It was an advertisement from a company, and their ad was about getting leads through divorces, and they had these books. I did edit the book and make it more personalized for my situation. I didn't write it from scratch. After going through a divorce and seeing the divorce rate up due to the pandemic with people stuck at home together, I felt it was important." She started her process during the pandemic. This was her response to "the pandemic is happening, and this is something I can do to help my situation." She added, "Also, I don't want anyone to have to go through the crap that I went through." This also fits with Rule Number 9.

Alicia told me that when she was forced to close her insurance office and work from home, it didn't affect the customers she had but made it much harder to get new customers. Because of that, she had a lot of extra time on her hands, so she started "spring cleaning" her house. While doing that, she kept coming across her old art supplies. She has always painted, but she had been too busy during the previous few years to do any painting. But with this extra time, she started painting again and has even sold some art, received a few requests for artwork, and is currently preparing for an art show with another artist. She said that after things get back to "normal," she will continue to paint. I am glad to hear this; I have seen some of her artwork that she posted on social media, and it is fantastic. The pandemic has given her a new lease on her hobby and turned it into something more! Alicia has turned her art hobby into a side hustle. (See Rule Number 3.)

Marisa used this time to improve her business by creating. "It actually gave me a lot more free time to get things done. People were typically hesitant to network virtually before the pandemic hit. They wanted to meet for lunch or coffee, and now we meet online. I already had everything in place to conduct business online, so that didn't change for me. I focused on my podcast and developed an online course. I took care of my existing customers. The online course is called *ACE Your Virtual Business* and is a collaboration between me and a veteran YouTuber. We've been working on it for almost a year now.

"Our first one is focusing on helping forty-plus people who are intimidated by technology to start a YouTube channel and a podcast. We will teach both and provide accountability and personal attention. We are launching our course with fifteen open seats so we can really help them on a personal level." By collaborating with someone, she is also exemplifying Rule Number 10.

One encouraging trend I have seen during the pandemic is many more people are becoming healthier. They are out walking and riding their bikes. One of my customers who owns a bike shop confirmed that more people are getting into the sport. While this won't necessarily change your financial position directly, it will change your health situation. That could give you more energy, which could possibly help your financial situation. So instead of sitting around, why not get out and create a healthier you while in this cocoon time? Exercise is also great for your attitude. (See Rule Number 11.)

Many of those who are walking are taking their dogs along or, in many cases, finding dogs to take along. I saw a story in *The Washington Post* that said, "Dog adoptions and sales are soaring during the pandemic. Shelters, rescues, and breeders report increased demand as Americans try to fill voids with canine companions." I also found an app called Walkzee that matches shelter dogs in need of a walk with dog lovers looking for a walking buddy. Having a pet to take care of can give you a sense of purpose, and this also helps your attitude.

Time will pass whether you do these things or not. Why not use this time to improve yourself so you can be better prepared for whatever life throws at you in the future? Like the butterfly, spread your wings and fly. While you are living in a cocoon, waiting for things to improve, it isn't much fun. But the results could be life changing!

Rule Number 2 Recap

In the Butterfly Model, we talked about what to do when it isn't currently possible to move forward because you have been sidelined by a closure or furlough/layoff. We listed many ways to prepare to move forward once you are able to. We listed examples like going back to school or just taking classes, remodeling your business, redoing your website, rewriting your operations manual, or creating a list of customers for later communication.

This situation is especially tough since you feel like you have no control. Doing some of the things in this chapter can give you back some of that control.

There are so many ways to prepare for the future. We also talked about the fact that time will pass whether you do these things or not, so why not come out ahead of where you are currently?

My contributors included their own examples about schooling, getting back to things they love, creating something new, remodeling, and using this time to set themselves up to succeed when they once again have the chance. Even getting more exercise would change things in the future for you.

The cocoon time might not be much fun, but it can bring you long-lasting results that could change your entire world.

DO THE WORK

How have you already used this rule in your life?

Can you add anything to this?

What idea(s) from this rule can you implement in your life?

1.

2.

3.

List your action steps to do this:

1.

2.

3.

RULE NUMBER 3

Everybody needs a side hustle— the Don't Put All Your Eggs in One Basket Model

NOTHING IS CONSTANT IN LIFE except change. This is the central belief of Heraclitus of Ephesus, the Greek philosopher. It basically means that nothing will stay the same forever. For the previous generation, it was normal for people to go to work for a single company and to retire from that company thirty-five or forty years later with a gold watch and a pension to support them for the rest of their life. That is a rare thing these days. Before I started my computer repair business, I had around ten different jobs. At some of them, I decided to leave; at others, that decision was made for me. I actually went through about ten years of underemployment and unemployment prior to going out on my own. From thebalancecareers.com, "The median number of years that wage and salary workers have worked for their current employer is currently 4.6 years, according to an Economic News Release from the Bureau of Labor Statistics. However, this longevity varies by age and occupation:

- The median tenure for workers age 25 to 34 is 3.2 years.

- The median tenure for employees age 65 and over is 10.3 years.

- Workers in management, professional, and related occupations had the highest median tenure (5.5 years).

- Workers in service occupations had the lowest median tenure (3.2 years)."

You may have a fantastic job that pays great today, but that can and probably will change at some point in your life, usually due to circumstances that are completely beyond your control. We have all learned that difficult lesson during the COVID-19 pandemic.

It is the same situation for businesses. Older people will remember how Blockbuster Video took over the world and sprouted up on almost every street corner decades ago. (I think

I still have my Blockbuster card somewhere.) The last I heard, there was one remaining store still open somewhere in Bend, Oregon. The rest have vanished. During its heyday, who would have thought that this, at the time, very successful business, with around 9,000 locations, would vanish? Hollywood Video had a similar history: it closed the very last of its 2,415 stores in July 2010 after a bankruptcy filing. These companies failed because they didn't see that the video world was changing. (See Rule Number 1). Just like the dinosaurs, they went away.

The retail world has quite a few similar examples. Do you remember Montgomery Ward, Circuit City, CompUSA, or

Foley's? Now Kmart, JCPenney, and Sears are going in a similar direction, along with many other retailers. Sears has survived for more than one hundred years. Did you know that from 1908 to the 1940s you could order a house out of the Sears catalog? Many of these houses are still around, but Sears continues to close more and more stores every year. Who would have thought twenty years ago that these huge, strong companies would all but disappear?

According to the website grammarist.com, "The expression side hustle was first used in 1950, which makes the term much older than many realize. The term became popular during and after the last recession, when traditional jobs disappeared and enterprising people had to make ends meet." That really is applicable to today's situation. But why wait for your job to disappear? Find a side hustle now, before you really need it. (See Rule Number 9.)

When I say side hustle, this could mean any number of things. I know many people who spend their evenings, weekends, and lunch hours working to build a multilevel marketing (MLM) business (Amway, SendOutCards, DōTERRA, Mary Kay, etc.) to either supplement their current income, or to hopefully replace it in the future. Many of these people have been successful during this pandemic since these companies all teach positive mental attitudes (see Rule Number 11) as one of the pillars of their business strategy.

I mentioned before that many people took to driving for the delivery services in their spare time to keep the lights on or just to gain some extra income or even to just get out of the house for a while. I saw an ad on Facebook recently: a mom was selling "Elf on the Shelf" kits. She put together twenty-four days of craft ideas and different or creative places to put the elf, along with the necessary props, and she was accepting preorders in early November so customers could have the kits in-hand before the Christmas holiday season had begun. While it is unlikely that this business model will replace other employment, it will probably pay for her Christmas or at least give her some extra money for a rainy day. (See Rule Number 8.)

An acquaintance of mine regularly gets a newsletter for LEGO enthusiasts that, among other things, lists all the LEGO sets that are being discontinued. If he thinks those sets will still be popular, he buys them up. (Many times, they end up on the clearance racks.) In a few months when they are discontinued and the demand is high, he sells them, for a premium, on eBay. He has used this extra money to send his family of seven to Disneyland a few times.

Speaking of eBay, there are countless stories of people using that platform and also Amazon and Shopify to create side businesses selling just about anything. There are plenty of books willing to teach you the ins and outs of this business. When you go to eBay and Amazon, most of the offerings are from small side hustle businesses.

It isn't always about making extra money. Many thriving businesses, including mine, started as a side hustle and grew to become the main source of income for their founders and often times for many employees also.

I started my computer repair business in 2010 as a side hustle while I was still working full time as a route salesman for a bread company. My working hours were very early in the morning, and I usually finished my route by noon, so I did the repair business in the afternoons and evenings after my route sales shift. My goal was to go full time in my business by 2015. I started my business on a shoestring. I didn't spend anything on advertising so, during those early years, I didn't make very much money from my business, but I did save all I made so I could get to full time sooner. (See Rule Number 8.) Two years later, in 2012, when that same bread company filed for bankruptcy and closed its doors, I made the decision to make my business full time. It was sooner than I had planned, so I am really glad I started that side hustle business when I did! When the bread company closed, I was six months away from being vested in its retirement plan, so I walked away from that job with absolutely nothing to show for the time I had put in.

A side hustle can be just about anything you are talented at, or passionate about, or even a potential career, but you just want to get your feet wet slowly to make sure it is what you are looking for. If you look online at Etsy, Pinterest, Shopify, Poshmark, or other similar sites, you will see plenty of side hustles. These are people who had created some type of hand-crafted items and decided to sell them. There are also the free-lance work sites such as Elance, Fiverr, Upwork, and many others. If you have writing, editing, graphic design, programming, or admin assistant skills, you can use these sites to capitalize on those skills. If you enjoy putting bookcases, tables, and other types of do-it-yourself furniture together, there is TaskRabbit and similar services.

There are also opportunities in childcare (Care.com, Sittercity.com, Helpr-app.com, SitterPro, and others), tutoring (tutors.com, wyzant.com, varsitytutors.com, and many others), and pet care (Rover.com, Wagwalking.com, and Pet Sitters International, to name a few). I had heard of only a couple of these sites, but after a quick internet search I found plenty of sites offering to help people find gigs. Unlike the side hustles listed in the previous paragraph, these can usually generate recurring customers and regularly scheduled sessions.

Paper routes are the original side hustle, but they are not even available in a lot of areas anymore. If your area still has a local newspaper, this could possibly be an option, and since it is usually done in the very early mornings, it probably wouldn't interfere with everything else you do. In my parents' city, there is a shortage of people wanting paper routes and that means getting the paper delivered is difficult. It might be like that in your community also. So this might be the opportunity you have been looking for. Most of these routes are "motor routes" now instead of "bicycle routes," so the work is not nearly as difficult as it was when my brothers and I had a few paper routes while growing up. Also, most now require prepayment for delivery, so you no longer have to go out every month and try to collect for the delivery like many of us had to do in the distant past. One of my paper routes was in a mobile home park, and there were times when I would go to deliver or collect for delivery and the whole house would be gone.

Do you have a great camera and an eye for photos? You could try your hand at photography and do family, high school graduates, baby, and wedding photos. I even know a guy who specializes in pet photography. Photography is much more difficult than it looks and might require some specialized editing software, so you might want some professional training before you attempt this. (See Rule Number 2.)

Having a side hustle doesn't have to mean some entrepreneurial quest or creative passion. Even getting a part-time job would be considered a side hustle. If you enjoy sports, most organized sports leagues rely on people with other full-time employment to act as referees for their games and tournaments. A quick Google search returned many options for the training needed, and most were less than one hundred dollars to get set up. Delivering pizza on weekends and evenings, bartending, being a barista, or being a restaurant server are other classic side hustles. The purpose of a side hustle is to save for the future. Don't spend your side hustle money frivolously.

The whole idea behind a side hustle is diversifying your income so if or when your main source of income goes away, you at least have something to fall back on. And before that happens you can save the side hustle money to improve your situation, pay some bills, and increase your safety net, just like I did. (See Rule Number 8.) We could all use some extra income.

If your side hustle is an entrepreneurial venture, you should research how different business structures can help you avoid paying more in income taxes. In *Rich Dad Poor Dad*, Robert Kiyosaki talks a lot about these structures to help people keep more of their business income. Another good book about this is *The Tax and Legal Playbook*, by Mark J. Kohler. I used the information in this book to learn how to save my business thousands per year by switching from a sole proprietor structure to an S corporation. Before I made the switch, I consulted with my accountant to make sure my thinking was correct and I was doing everything legally and by the book. As with anything else, if you need to invest any money or sign any contracts for your new side hustle, it is best to get professional advice first. (See Rule Number 10.)

As a business, you can add to the mix and kind of create a side hustle. I know of a gym that decided since it had to close down when the government deemed it was too dangerous to go work out with others in close proximity, it would rent out its barbells, mats, and any other handheld equipment to members. Since the owners already had their customers' contact information (see Rule Number 6), they decided to contact all their customers and offer to rent these items out to them because they could not currently come to the gym. They got a great response from their customers, and they even purchased more equipment to keep their customers working out at home. This paragraph could fit into many of the chapters in this book; it is a great idea. If you own a business, are there items you could possibly rent out or use in another way if, or when, things get shut down again? Thinking about these things now and being prepared will make a world of difference next time. Until that happens, it could create another income stream for your business.

Rule Number 3 Recap

Everything changes; nothing stays the same. This is especially true in the work world. For past generations, it was normal to go to work for a single company and spend your entire career there. That is very rare these days. You can no longer count on one employer to keep you going until retirement. You must watch out for yourself.

One way to do that is with a side hustle. I mentioned many side hustle ideas. They come in just about any category you can think of: entrepreneurship, creative endeavors, part-time work, or a possible new career. The possibilities are endless. If you are interested in a certain type of side hustle, do some research and you can find many ways to get involved in it. The important thing is to create an extra stream of income so in case your main source goes away, you still have something to fall back on.

We talked about Blockbuster and other video stores that didn't see that things were changing and paid the ultimate price. We also talked about retailers that have been around for longer than most of us have been alive but now can't compete and are disappearing. This chapter gives you many ideas to put in place before your company goes down that same road.

We talked about the fact that many side hustles have turned into full-time gigs for many founders and now they have added employees to their ranks, which also helps those people. We even mentioned a business that created a sort of side hustle to keep business going during the shutdowns.

DO THE WORK

How have you already used this rule in your life?

Can you add anything to this?

What idea(s) from this rule can you implement in your life?

1.

2.

3.

List your action steps to do this:

1.

2.

3.

RULE NUMBER 4

Look for recurring revenue—
the Life Insurance Sales Model

ONE OF THE GREAT THINGS about selling life insurance, or many other commission sales jobs, has always been the recurring revenue. You sell a policy or service once, and as long as the buyer keeps making those monthly premiums or payments, you will continue to get paid every month also. I am not advocating that everyone should start selling life insurance, but we should all be looking for opportunities where we can continue to get paid for a product or service we have already sold or would have sold anyway.

If you often refer your customers to certain products or services that you don't currently sell, you should look into affiliate or partner programs for those products or services. Usually, services are more matched to this strategy, or products that are often reordered frequently, such as supplies that keep getting used up. It never hurts to ask, and if you are recommending these companies because they are top-notch, there is no ethical reason not to try to get a piece of the action. Imagine if you could get an ongoing small portion of the money you make for others. You never know—they might discover your great ability to sell their products or services and attempt to hire you full time.

This is similar to the consumer advertisements that we all get from time to time for services we use, such as TV services, credit cards, or cell phone companies, which will, for example, pay us fifty dollars if we recommend the service to our friends and our friends sign up. With these consumer plans, we will never get ahead—just make maybe enough for a dinner out. But the core idea is the same.

After many years of recommending great products and services to many of my customers, I have finally embraced this rule in my business, and I have set a goal to eventually be able to cover all my personal expenses with this type of recurring revenue. I have been evaluating everything I recommend to my customers to see if there is some type of revenue-sharing possible with those companies. Some don't have programs, but many do. Look for partner programs, resellers, or something similar on their websites. Even if they don't list this on their website, just ask if they do this. Just to be clear, I have not changed the way I recommend products to my customers. I have just made it possible to get paid sometimes if I recommend certain companies. In most cases, it is really simple to do this. Companies usually give me a personal link that I use when setting up this product over the internet for my customer. There is no extra paperwork. I also make sure my customers are aware that I do get a cut from the company they are buying from. (It also doesn't affect the amount they pay for the product or service.) This is absolutely a win for my customers who use these services, for my suppliers that offer these incentives, and for me. In just a few months, I have created enough recurring revenue to consistently make my monthly car payment. So this helps me with Rule Number 8 also.

Since I own my business, I have also been able to become a distributor for a few companies that I was already recommending to my customers. I am able to purchase the distributors' products at a discount and then sell them to my customers at the advertised price. Like I said before, I would recommend these products anyway, but now I get a part of the profit for my recommendation. Doing this has added a few thousand dollars to my bottom line each year while I'm doing basically the same thing. It has also required me to get a sales tax license and collect sales tax on all these sales, so it is important to research all sides when adding something to your business. The sales tax returns take only a few minutes each quarter, and I have my accountant do the paperwork. Even with this extra expense, it was a good addition for my business. Using this strategy, I made an additional $3,000 in the last six months.

A strategy similar to the one above involves rebates. Many companies offer rebates to their customers. Many roofing companies get rebates from certain shingle companies, and I know many other industries do this also. If you purchase a lot of products, check to see if there are rebates available from your suppliers. I don't purchase a lot of the same things over and over, but occasionally I get a rebate for computer parts I purchase. The paperwork usually takes only a few minutes, and the rewards can add up.

My friend, Christy, is an excellent business networker and highly regarded as a "business connector." According to Medium.com, "*Business Connectors* are the people who know large numbers of people and who are in the habit of making introductions. They usually know people across an array of social, cultural, professional, and economical circles, and make a habit of introducing people who work or live in different circles. They are people who link us up with the world, people with a special gift for bringing the world together."

Christy recently told me about a colleague of hers who has partnered with a networking business and is trying to grow this business in our area. Christy has referred many people to her, because that is what Christy does. This person has started offering Christy a kickback for anyone she sends to her who signs up for her group. Christy wasn't looking for an opportunity like this, but since she is an excellent networker, this opportunity found her. She is able to do this in the normal course of her day, hasn't changed how she does things, and now gets paid a little for it. She actually has another business that gives her SPIFs (sales performance incentive funds) for recommending its barter service in her area. These two activities probably won't replace her full-time work, but the income does add up and helps her save for a rainy day. (See Rule Number 8.)

Do you have special knowledge or a skill, or maybe just something that needs to be said, that you can teach or pass on to others through videos or by writing a book? It is becoming easier all the time to post videos or self-publish a book. Once the work is done, you can possibly earn ongoing income with some added marketing efforts. Marisa did this by creating her online course and starting her weekly podcast.

Monika has a customer whose business was mostly shut down because it was in the travel industry, so she started making YouTube videos with her kids about "things to do since the kids are not in school." After only a few months, they have gained more than 800 subscribers and they are getting close to being able to monetize their YouTube account. (From your-business.azcentral.com, "Monetize is the term YouTube uses for its official program that allows users to make money from the clips they upload. YouTube has strict criteria for which clips are eligible to make money. For those which are eligible, the uploader can share in revenue from advertisements shown before, during, or alongside the clip.")

You can actually get paid by some social media sites if your content gets enough attention and you become an influencer. Also, some companies will pay you to talk about their products (affiliate marketing). This is definitely not an overnight thing. It could take years, and many people attempt this, while only a few of them ever make it big. But if this is your passion, at least you will enjoy the ride and maybe get some free products along the way.

If you provide any ongoing services, you should at least have your customers on a contract. This allows you to know how much is coming in on a regular basis and actually plan or budget for it. (See Rule Number 8). It also ensures that you and your customers are both on the same page about what you are doing for them and when you are going to do it. For business owners, this is sort of like getting a regular paycheck.

This is what Monika does with her social media customers: "When I work with people on their social media, I put them on a contract so that it is recurring every month, it is my base, and then I get other projects, but those others, I can't always count on. It isn't passive income, but it is predictable." When you work for yourself, that means a lot.

The whole idea behind this rule is to make more money without having to do more work. Many industries offer these kinds of incentives. An internet search could possibly help you find some partners, or maybe you could ask others in your industry if they do this or if they know of companies that offer this. (See Rule Number 10.) The time you spend researching this could be well worth it.

Rule Number 4 Recap

This chapter was all about working smarter and not harder. Recurring revenue is something that can really increase your results with no extra effort. We all work very hard, and having a way to earn more while not working more would go a long way toward becoming and staying essential in the future. In this chapter, we gave a number of examples of people who are using this and also ways to incorporate this into your own work. The possibilities are endless. If you deal with recommending anything to your customers that you don't sell or represent, you need to find a way to get part of this transaction for yourself. We talked about the words to look for to find these types of programs: partner, reseller, affiliate, distributor. If you don't see any of these, just ask if the company does this.

I told you how I have added this to my business and how it has quickly made a difference in my finances. I also showed how some others have used this too. As in Christy's case, it doesn't even have to be connected to your company.

We also talked about making sure the product or service is top-notch and you would recommend it regardless of whether the company was paying you or not. It is also important that your customer is not paying extra just so you can get paid. This works best when everyone is winning.

DO THE WORK

How have you already used this rule in your life?

Can you add anything to this?

What idea(s) from this rule can you implement in your life?

1.

2.

3.

List your action steps to do this:

1.

2.

3.

RULE NUMBER 5

Make money while you sleep—the Self-Service Car Wash Model

AM I SAYING YOU SHOULD go out and purchase a self-service car wash? Not necessarily, but they can be highly profitable, and who wouldn't want to make money while they sleep? Most of the ideas attached to this rule might require some type of financial investment. Please always check out any company thoroughly and also run it by your financial advisor, accountant, and attorney before sending anyone any money or even signing any paperwork or contracts. (See Rule Number 10.) Also see my comments in the last paragraph of Rule Number 3 about tax-savings strategies. There is no point in making extra money if you are going to give it all to the government in taxes.

Self-service car washes are typically open twenty-four hours per day, seven days per week, and don't require constant supervision. So you really could make money while you sleep. Many times, I have driven by a self-service car wash late at night and saw someone there washing a car. I know that seems a little creepy, but it happens. Another similar business is self-service laundromats, although they do require quite a bit more attention and have more machinery that could break down. But weather is not a factor for them like it is with a car wash. Either of these you could easily work into your busy schedule, since very little supervision is required. You could also hire someone for the upkeep on this type of business. Just make sure you have business processes in place to keep that person honest.

The idea of making money while you sleep is really about finding ways for your money to work for you. If you have some money to invest, this is a definite possibility. While watching *Shark Tank*, I have seen Kevin O'Leary (Mr. Wonderful) many times talking about the investments he is considering. He calls his money his "little soldiers" that he is sending out, and he expects them to come back home soon and to bring friends with them. Most of the book, *Rich Dad Poor Dad*, by Robert Kiyosaki is about this model and acquiring assets and putting them to work for you. There are only so many hours that you can work, but your money can always be working. It never gets tired. As your money grows, it will work harder and harder for you.

If a self-service car wash or laundromat is not for you, there are many other types of businesses that don't require a lot of supervision. It is possible to find "turnkey" businesses that can be mostly owner-absent. According to Investopedia, "A turnkey business is a business that is ready to use, existing in a condition that allows for immediate operation. The term 'turnkey' is based on the concept of only needing to turn the key to unlock the doors to begin operations." Some franchises are advertised this way. I have known a few people who owned hair salons or nail salons and didn't know the first thing about how to cut, perm, or color hair, or do nails, but they did know how to hire the right people who would handle all of that for them. One person I know of didn't even live in the same state as his salon.

While a lot of these businesses are not as popular today as they once were, they still fit the model, so I will list them. Some might not even be available any longer, but they still might give you other ideas. When I was growing up, I remember my grandfather had a number of coin-operated gumball, nut, and candy machines in his garage. He had made agreements with different stores and businesses that allowed him to place these machines in high-traffic areas, and he would give the store owners a small portion of the profits in exchange. He only had to go by every so often and restock the machines, clean them up, make any repairs to broken machines, and remove the money. I have known many others who did the same thing with soda pop machines, video games, pinball machines, and tire pump air machines. If you own a restaurant or a bar, adding an arcade machine could give you extra revenue from a corner that now sits empty. You could also add a soda pop machine at your self-service car wash or laundromat. Any kind of vending machine would work for this.

Pay telephones used to fit into this category. I remember seeing many ads for these as investments in the eighties, after deregulation of the phone system. I am so glad I passed on those, because cell phones have rendered them almost entirely useless. Speaking of newer technology, it is possible to create websites and make money from advertising other sites on your site. This takes a lot of knowledge of SEO and other marketing techniques, so some training and research would be in order before going down this road. (See Rule Number 2.) But if you can build the sites yourself, the initial cost could be pretty small.

Rental real estate definitely falls into this category too. You can own a house, condo, duplex, apartment building, or commercial property and someone else is paying the mortgage and many times even giving you some monthly income as well. You can even hire a professional property management service so you don't have to deal with finding renters, mowing lawns, fixing broken pipes, or other tenant or maintenance issues. However, some landlords have been worried lately about not being able to evict tenants for nonpayment during the pandemic. So you may need to have strong financial reserves if you want to pursue this idea.

Another real estate idea is fix-and-flips; this is where you purchase distressed properties and fix them up and then sell them for a profit. There are a few reality television shows about this for reference. Even during the pandemic, people are still buying and selling houses. In fact, there might be more opportunities for inexpensive properties now, due to foreclosures. There are many books that can teach you how to make extra money in real estate. In Robert Kiyosaki's book, *Rich Dad Poor Dad*, he spends a lot of time talking about how he made some of his fortune using real estate, and not always in the conventional ways that you might think.

This next example isn't really making money while you sleep, but it is making money in your business while at your current job, so I will include it here. Gary is a business broker, and he has talked to many people with full-time jobs who are now working remotely, so they are looking to purchase businesses. "I also think there are a lot of people who want to buy a business as a side business because they are working at home. I sold a salad business to two ladies; one of them is going to run it day to day, and the other one is currently working remotely so she can do her job at the restaurant location and work both jobs. I think the ability to work remotely has opened up the opportunity for people to buy businesses and run two businesses parallel." This is definitely putting your money to work for you.

Gary also told me about another customer of his who is currently a marketing VP of a company. This VP is buying a printing business, and since he is working remotely, he can do his marketing job from his office in his new printing company while overseeing this new printing operation.

One of the big draws to MLMs is the duplication (teaching others to do what you do) and the act of recruiting and growing a team, and that fits with this rule. Nina told me "part of this business is growing a team. That is part of how we make our income, so while I may not be having any wine tastings today, I have forty or fifty people on my team who are having tastings, so I am making money no matter what." That is kind of like making money while you sleep, but even better because you can have multiple people making money for you while you sleep. They are actually multiplying instead of duplicating her efforts.

Lynn told me, "As a business owner, you might be at a meeting, but you are still making money since you have employees working while you are out. It's like this: I am going to have a really good day today while sitting here having Zooms all day because three of my best stylists are totally booked."

Rule Number 5 Recap

The Self-Service Car Wash Model is all about making your money work for you. We talked about many different types of investments, mostly in money but a few in time, that can end up working for you and hopefully replace some or all of your earned income. This chapter can be a pivotal part of your overall plan to become essential. There are different degrees of involvement with these investments, and that is also something to consider. While a self-service car wash might not take much time, the investment might require more than a turnkey business. You need to weigh the possibilities and the return on investment these businesses could give you.

The ideas listed require some investment, and if you are not able to do this currently, you should use some of the other rules to get to the point where you can take advantage of this rule. This chapter alone could make you essential so you don't have to worry about your job again.

DO THE WORK

How have you already used this rule in your life?

Can you add anything to this?

What idea(s) from this rule can you implement in your life?

1.

2.

3.

List your action steps to do this:

1.

2.

3.

RULE NUMBER 6

Stay on your customers' radar— the Top-of-Mind Model

IN MY INTRODUCTION, I mentioned the Ostrich Model, where you bury your head in the sand and hope for the best. The businesses and individuals who do that will find that when they finally pull their heads out of the sand, the world has passed them by. Things might get tough, but people still need the same products and services. If their previous suppliers are closed or just not paying attention, you just have to let them know about yourself so you can offer to help them. (See Rule Number 9.)

This could also be called the "communication model," because that is essentially what it is all about. I have talked to many businesses that started keeping their customers up to date on what was going on with their company during the uncertainty of closures, running at very small capacity, and shortened hours, etc. Some took to email, while others used social media, postcards, SendOutCards, and even signs or banners on their windows or in front of their businesses. There were even businesses that started using text messages to communicate to their customers. The common denominator was that they continued to communicate with their customers. They did this in an informational and nonsales manner.

I heard a story once about an old woman who asked her husband one day, "How come you never tell me that you love me anymore?" His reply was, "I told you once, and if I change my mind, I will let you know." She didn't appreciate his lack of communication, and I am sure your customers wouldn't either.

There can be a lot of uncertainty when everything is closed, and you don't know if your favorite companies will make it or not. The companies that communicate will always fare much better than those that don't. It keeps you "top of mind" with your customers. It also keeps the rumors about your business shutting down for good from gaining a life of their own. If you don't have a list of your customers' email addresses, mailing addresses, or phone numbers, you should begin to compile a list as you meet with any customers in the future. It is never too late to start. If you tell your customers the list is just to keep them informed and not to sell them anything, they will be happy to give you this information.

Sending any communication to your customers helps. Some years, I have sent out Christmas cards to all my customers and other years I got behind and didn't get it done. Each time I did send out the cards, I received a few calls shortly after that from customers saying they had lost my business card and were really glad I sent the Christmas card. Each time I send them out, the cards pay for themselves with these types of responses and new appointments from them. I know of a dentist's office that sends out fun but informative birthday cards to customers on their birthday. That helps keep the office "top of mind."

To keep customers informed and even build business, Nina, the wine tasting consultant, said, "This was really pivotal in the beginning because I was servicing my customers, letting them know that I was still out there until I figured out how to revamp my business. Contrary to what you might think, in the beginning I was not doing great. People were going to the liquor store, but they were not buying from me until I started figuring out how to make the pivot. I think when we get in that desperation mode, people can smell it. So, once I started having fun and I was no longer desperate, it turned around."

Nina started using Facebook events. "Over a couple days, we would talk about the different specials that we had and the different wines that we had, and then we had like a twenty-minute live gathering, and after that people could post online that they wanted to order. So, we had to be really innovative in that respect."

My chiropractor, Skylar, ended up in a very difficult situation right at the beginning of the pandemic. He was informed that the office he had rented just a few months before was not zoned for a medical office. He was forced to immediately close his new office. He quickly got in touch with a colleague in a nearby office and temporarily moved his practice into his colleague's office. Since he had all the contact information for his customers, he was able to properly communicate the office change, and he didn't miss a single appointment. He stayed in that office for a couple months while looking for a new office space. Once he found one, he again contacted all his customers and moved everything to his new office. Now, a few months into his, hopefully permanent, office he has actually grown his customer base. Since he used great communication, none of his customers were concerned about the many moves and he is doing great! He also used Rule Number 10 by asking a colleague for help.

Communication is extremely important for individuals too. I have heard some people say that they don't like having meetings on Zoom or Microsoft Teams, so they tend to stay away from them unless they are specifically required to attend. This might have been fine for the first few weeks, but as time goes on, these folks are getting further and further behind those of us who continue to meet up with our existing contacts and even make new contacts in this virtual new world.

Yes, I said make new contacts. Many people have been using social media to find like-minded individuals or people who might benefit from their products or services, and then they moved beyond email and messaging and started meeting on video where they could start a real business relationship.

This also means if your products or services can be purchased and serviced in other parts of the country or even the world, this could open up new markets for you. (See Rule Number 1, Status quo.) When I started conducting interviews for this book, one of the questions I asked was, "Who do you know that I should know?" I was able to meet some new people and interview them for my book. I am sure some of them will become customers of mine, or business associates of some kind.

This is what Nina discovered. She has now had many virtual tastings with participants from different states all in the same virtual tasting. This will be a popular option for her business going forward, which will help her business grow.

I belong to a number of groups that used to meet weekly or monthly in person for the purpose of networking with other business owners. During the pandemic, all these groups have moved to Zoom. While the number of participants is down in some of the groups, you can truly see who is fighting for their livelihood and who is doing the ostrich impersonation. I even belong to groups that have taken on a number of new members because people recognize the importance of staying on the radar and even expanding their reach. If you have more time due to not being able to work at 100 percent or having less drive time, you should invest that time into meeting new people. (See Rule Number 2.) It is also good for your mental health and possibly your bottom line. If you want to find groups near you, you can look online at Meetup.com. That site has thousands of groups in every imaginable category for business or even hobbies.

A couple of my groups have started using the breakout rooms feature in Zoom. That is where, instead of one big group of maybe twenty or even thirty people or more, the host breaks the group into many small groups of three or four people and gives them a few minutes to talk in those "rooms." Then, all participants return to the main "room," and the host randomly breaks everyone out again. This kind of mimics actual mingling in an in-person event. The only difference is that you don't get to choose who is in the breakout room with you, but this is actually better than choosing which participants you talk to.

I was discussing this with a friend the other day, and he commented that these breakout rooms have really opened his eyes. They have shown him that he has not been using networking to its full potential in person. He, like many of us, was in the habit of showing up and spending most of his time talking with the people he already had relationships with, but the breakout rooms have forced him to step out of his comfort zone and talk to others he might not know. He really sees the value in this and told me he will try much harder to meet everyone in the room when things get back to in-person networking again.

About talking to everyone in networking meetings, Lynn had this to say: "I learned that probably ten years ago while networking with a friend. She told me, 'Don't talk to me and hang out with me. Go talk to some new people. That is why we are here.' She made me do this for about the first year I did networking, so now I walk in and I see everyone I know, and I want to go catch up with them, but first I need to meet all the other people. That is why I try to arrive early and leave late to catch everyone. I try to show up everywhere so I can stay top of mind with everyone. They may have a hair stylist now, but that can change, and I want them to think of me if it does.

"Similar to networking is checking in daily when I get to my salon. It takes like ten seconds—you know, something like "Hair all day." I really just use my Facebook page for my business; I have a bunch of older customers who are Facebook friends, so I make sure not to post anything inappropriate or controversial."

The next step in this type of business communication is to set up a one-on-one meeting, either virtually or in person with these people you meet so you can get to know them better and create a real business relationship with them. It isn't all about trying to find customers for your business. You might discover that you need their services or products, or they might become a strategic partner for your business.

I have even heard of assisted living centers where some of the residents will open their doors and sit in their doorways at a safe distance and talk to each other in the hallway just so they can have some human interaction. We are all social creatures; we need to have a connection with others.

Another part of communication is regularly staying in contact with your customers. BK, my mortgage broker friend, has kept up his daily calls to try to build his business. (See rule Number 9.) During the pandemic, he noticed that many in his industry were not keeping up with their current customers (realtors). Since he was still making these calls on a daily basis, he was getting the opportunity to handle loans for realtors he had not been able to work with before the pandemic. He heard many times that they normally get eight to ten calls from mortgage brokers per week but now the only calls they were receiving were from him.

BK was in the habit of meeting face to face with many prospects on a weekly basis. He quickly realized that he needed to shift to Zoom and try to make those connections as personal as possible by making sure he had good eye contact. He tried to make the Zoom meetings fun so people would want to continue to participate in them.

Don't forget to thank those customers who support your business. This is probably one of the most important types of communication. When you thank them, be sincere and specific if you can. If you are in an industry that normally doesn't send out thank-you notes, you will definitely be remembered. This doesn't require a lot of time but can make a big difference. I know many business owners who use SendOutCards for this because it allows you to add a gift, like some cookies or brownies. I have been sending out thank-you letters to my new customers every month since I started my business. I include a couple more business cards in case the customer lost my card. This sometimes gets me new referrals from these customers. I also send them another letter one year later if they have not used my services again. You have to stay top of mind with your customers. Since I am very busy these days, I have a virtual assistant that sends out these letters for me. (See Rule Number 10.)

It is also wise to keep your hours and days of operation up to date on your website and also on Google My Business and your business Facebook page. If you have a storefront, you should make sure your hours are updated there also. You want your current and potential customers to conveniently find you and not show up when you are closed.

Rule Number 6 Recap

This rule is all about communication, with your customers, your suppliers, your potential customers, and even in your personal life. A lack of communication can leave your customers thinking you have closed for good. We talked about the many ways to communicate with these people and the fact that skipping virtual meetings because you don't like them or are tired of them is a bad idea and could leave you left out in the future.

If you use networking as a source of leads in your business, it is also really important to continue networking even if you can't do it in person. After these meetings, don't forget to follow up with those who you met to keep the conversation going.

Thanking your customers is another important part of communication, especially in types of business where thanking is not common. This can really make you stand out.

Finally, we talked about keeping your hours of operation up to date. When things can change on a daily basis, it is important to let everyone know about those changes, whether it was your idea, or you were forced to make the changes.

DO THE WORK

How have you already used this rule in your life?

Can you add anything to this?

What idea(s) from this rule can you implement in your life?

1.

2.

3.

List your action steps to do this:

1.

2.

3.

RULE NUMBER 7

Search for what isn't being done— the Outside the Box Model

THIS RULE IS ALL ABOUT solving problems. If your business model no longer works, or your job has gone away, you need to solve that problem. During the pandemic, there were many people trying to solve problems, and some of them have found a new lease on life because of it.

Inventors are created every day. While there are some who invent item after item, many inventors create only one or two inventions. These are not super high-IQ geniuses who are doing this inventing. Most of the time, it is an average man or woman who looks at something and says, "There must be a better way," and then comes up with that better way.

Have you ever thought about a better way of doing something or creating something to solve a problem you have? You could be an inventor. If you have ever watched *Shark Tank*, the show where inventors and new business owners try to get multimillionaire investors to invest in their ideas, you have probably seen what is possible as an inventor. If you listen to their stories, many were simply trying to solve their own problems and hit on a great idea. Now they have businesses that can sustain them and make sure they remain "essential."

Scientists have come up with testing kits, and programmers have come up with apps to help track infections and other statistics from COVID-19. There were also people who created better masks that were more comfortable and came in designer colors and patterns. I heard about several distilleries that started making alcohol-based hand sanitizer when the regular suppliers could not keep up with the demand. Their businesses were still operating, but they realized they could supply a much-needed product, so they temporarily made the switch. This also applies to Rule Number 10, because they saw an opportunity to help their neighbors. This might get them some goodwill in the future. I know in a lot of places, it at least got them mentioned on the news.

This doesn't have to be a product. Is there a service you think is needed but not available in your area? Years ago, my niece started a drop-off laundry business at her house. She was a stay-at-home mom with three young kids, so working outside the home would not work for her. She printed up flyers and posted them in business areas of her city, and created a

Facebook page, and did a little advertising. She did this business for about three years while her kids were very young.

My business has fared well during the pandemic, because it is in the "essential" category since I deal with computers and IT, but it has made me change how I do things to some degree. I don't have a shop; my business is mobile, so I usually go to my customers' home or office and work on their computers there. But since we were supposed to associate only with people in our immediate household, I have had to do some things differently. I had a customer who wanted me to set up his new laptop for him. He left the laptop in a hidden box on his front porch, and I drove by and picked it up. I took it home and did all the setup and even downloaded printer drivers. Then I drove back to his house, pulled into the driveway where I connected his laptop to his wifi, and proceeded to set up his printers and scanner from there while on the phone with him, making sure the printers and scanner worked. He wasn't comfortable with me being in his house, so this was a way to complete the setup while keeping our distance. I have also had many customers who either dropped off their computer on my porch, or I picked it up from their porch to complete the repairs. I have even worked on a few computers in my car while my customers were in their car a few spaces away in a parking lot. All I needed was a power inverter and a wifi hotspot.

Prior to the pandemic, like most people, I had never used Zoom. I had to quickly learn how to use it and become an expert on it, because I had many customers contacting me to help them figure it out. Rather than lose those customers, I had to "invent" a process to be able to teach these people how to use it. I would remote into their computer and then send them a Zoom invite and walk them through the entire process of following the link for getting on the Zoom meeting and making sure their camera and microphone were working. I would even walk them through screen sharing and using the message feature. It was almost like I was in the same room with them looking over their shoulder.

In my town, a company started delivering from the local liquor stores, so folks didn't have to go out to those stores. I am sure that has happened in a lot of places. There have also been some bars that will allow you to buy an unmade drink online and they will deliver the ingredients to your door and then, at a designated time, they do a Zoom meeting and teach you how to make the drink during their "Virtual Happy Hour." This keeps their customers engaged with the bar and each other, even if they can't come to the bar. (See Rule Number 6.)

I have heard of restaurants with large parking lots that turned them into drive-in movie theaters so people could still get dinner and a movie while they stayed socially distant. Many large churches are also holding services in their parking lots with the members in their cars and the preacher on the roof of the church so he can be easily seen and heard. Many churches are also doing Facebook Live for their services to keep their congregations involved. My parents used to meet in person each week with some friends to have a Bible study. When they were no longer able to meet up, they all got webcams, and now they meet up on Zoom each week. It may not be as good as meeting in person, but their meetings sometimes last close to two hours on Zoom because they all enjoy just talking.

My son has "attended" two concerts in the past few months. Both were virtual since large crowds were not allowed anywhere yet. At the first one, the artists were sitting on a stool or standing in a room just playing their instruments and singing. My son said it was like watching a YouTube video—not very exciting or even worth the price of the ticket. The second one was a multimedia sensation. The artists said they were trying to make it something special and, in fact, they did. There were times when the artists were swinging in the air from wires, appeared to be walking on lasers, and doing other surprising things. Concertgoers could tap one button on their computers for applause and another for screams. All other attendees could hear when the other attendees were tapping out applause or screaming, just like at a real concert. They could also watch the concert from many different views: up front, way in the back, even behind the scenes. Three of the members of this band were brothers, and they even included a camera that showed their father's reaction while watching the concert, "the Gary Cam."

The attendees were not just spectators but participants. My son said he would love to do a concert like this again. He probably won't go to another concert for the first artists again. The second group of artists realized they had an opportunity to make something very special. They got creative, and their fans really loved what they created. It wasn't the same old thing; they invented a new way to do concerts.

This second band also had "virtual tables" set up, and they were selling T-shirts, posters, and other merchandise, just like at a live concert. My son was able to get a T-shirt, a poster, and a program ordered, so he can add them to his collection just like at a live concert.

Miranda, the journalist, told me about some businesses she interviewed. She talked to owners of an escape room who obviously couldn't do their normal business since they were not able to open their doors, so they came up with "to go" escape room crates they rent out. They already had these crates for the past few years and would lend them to schools to help the kids improve their math and critical thinking skills, but now they are using them to keep their doors open, so to speak. They started out with ten crates and one theme but have since added more themes. They said the crates are being rented out every day, and when they are returned, the crates are taken apart and completely sanitized for the next customer. They reported, "People have really enjoyed these."

Miranda also talked with owners of a crafting company that normally has people come in with groups and create DIY projects. But now they are assembling take-home kits: things like home décor signs to paint or backyard games like Giant Jenga. She said their customers love the kits; they encourage people to get the kits and then do the crafting over Zoom with friends. They have even been asked if they will continue the take-home kits after the pandemic is over. So this could actually expand their business capacity in the future by adding the kits to their mix. (See Rule Number 1, adding to the mix).

Miranda also had to figure out new ways to do her job, since she could not go to many places for her interviews and wasn't even able to go into the studio for the nightly news shows. She has been conducting most of her interviews over Zoom or outside and keeping a safe distance and broadcasting her stories live from her living room. She said occasionally her two cats make it into the newscast. She is fortunate that she doesn't have small children to get in the broadcasts and her husband doesn't work from home. I have seen some newscasters who had to use a closet for their broadcasts because their houses were full of kids and spouses who were also working or attending school from home.

When offices were first being shut down, I received many calls from businesses asking me how they could keep their employees connected to the office while working at home. I set up many offices with systems that keep them in business and able to communicate immediately with each other just like they used to when they were in the same office. Some of these businesses might never go back to the office 100 percent. The important thing is that they didn't give up; they searched for a way to continue doing business by calling me. (See Rule Number 10.)

Nina found a new way to do her wine tastings. "Here is where it really started to turn for me. I found that [a way to keep doing business] by creating experiences for people, especially since we were about four or five months in. People had been locked down, they were isolated, and they were craving human interactions. The experiences were cocktail wine making. Who wouldn't like to learn how to make cocktails from wine? So they would prepurchase the wines that we would make the cocktails with and have them delivered to their home, so now I have the sales up front instead of at the end. Then, I would send them the ingredients they would need for the cocktail making. Then we would virtually get together on Zoom and make the cocktails together. So I would tell them already up front, 'Have chopped-up limes; have lemon juice.' These were simple ingredients, but it was very fun and very interactive. Take that a step further; we started doing charcuterie making. So interactive: 'This is how you make the little flowers out of salami. This is how you cut the strawberries to make them look like roses.'

"People would prepurchase their wines and then they would pair those wines with the charcuterie they were making. We also did virtual wine tastings with our wine maker as well. The experiences have really taken off. We have done fondue, charcuterie, cocktails, wine trivia, and even scavenger hunts. Those have been used as team builders for companies. While they may not have been able to do their company party, they could put together this fun activity as a team-building event. So we were able to talk to people and say, 'What kind of experience would you like for your friends?' And we could build that experience around you.

"The other side of the virtual wine tasting is that it is bringing people together from all over the country. We could get a group of sorority girls who all lived in different states, or family members in different states. You choose the wines that you want everyone to taste, and they are prepurchased and shipped to everyone's homes, and then we all jump onto Zoom at the same time and all taste the selections together. Now this has been fun, because people are connecting with people they haven't seen in years from all over the country."

She has worked with groups of neighbors, but they were all social distancing, so the host would buy the samples and separate them into Jell-O shot cups for each participant and leave them on her porch for the neighbors to come by and pick up their samples. Then, when everyone had them, they Zoomed into the tasting. "People don't want to get on one more Zoom call and just stare at everyone, so the events have been popular," Nina reported.

"Once everything goes back to normal, we will continue to do this. Since we have added this new skill, it has opened up the door to do business in other states. It has also been a great tool for recruiting. Some people have been furloughed, or they have lost their job, and they need the extra income. If they are in food service, they are not making as much money as they were making before. Many people are realizing they can do this business from home; they don't have to get in their car and go somewhere. I can do business this way. It has opened up a new door for them.

"Pre COVID-19, I was doing six to eight tastings per month, and now I am doing eight to twelve, and now 90 percent of them are in person. I think in this we come out so much stronger. At this point, we become survivors. It has been such an eye-opener, because we get tunnel vision. We all fall into the trap of, 'That's how we have always done it.'"

Lynn had just dropped her franchise name in January 2020 and was just starting to rebrand her salon. Here is what she did to reinvent her company: "I just rebranded my business and got rid of the franchise name in January 2020, so my business is really brand new. Everything in my advertising used to be Valpak and advertising in some magazines, and since COVID-19, I haven't been doing those things yet with the new business. I pay $25 to $30 per month in Facebook ads, and I can reach 30,000 people. I am getting $150 to $200 per day from new customers off of Facebook. And then it also goes over to Instagram. All of my current advertising is from social media.

"As for reinventing my business, marketing is my passion. I spend a lot of time in Facebook groups with other salons. I am always looking at what salons in Chicago are doing, for example, or even other salons in Parker. What can I do that they are not doing? I am in probably forty different Facebook groups of hair salon owners and they ask questions like, 'What are you doing during the pandemic? How are you getting customers?' I get so many ideas from these. I use these groups to research ideas to keep things moving.

"I am also really glad I dropped the franchise, because that would have cost me $35,000 last year, and that might have killed my business."

As you can see, there are many ways to do things different from how they have always been done. Look at what you have always done, and see if you can think outside the box and find a new way to stay relevant in your job or business.

Rule Number 7 Recap

This chapter concentrated on solving problems. We talked about inventors who got started by thinking, "There must be a better way," and then they found that way to solve not only their own problem, but a problem for many people. We talked about the fact that this doesn't have to be a product. You might create a new service that solves a problem for many.

We gave examples of how different people created something new in their businesses or better ways to do things. If you can't do things the way you used to do them, then you need to find a new way if you want to keep doing your business. Thinking outside the box can be applied to anything: concerts, restaurants, bars, retail stores, escape rooms, service businesses. The possibilities are endless.

Many of the people interviewed mentioned that these new ideas will make their business much stronger in the future because they have new ways to interact with their customers.

DO THE WORK

How have you already used this rule in your life?

Can you add anything to this?

What idea(s) from this rule can you implement in your life?

1.

2.

3.

List your action steps to do this:

1.

2.

3.

RULE NUMBER 8

Live beneath your means—
The Rainy Day Model

DURING THE INITIAL FIRST WEEKS of the pandemic, when most businesses were closed and public health officials were asking people to not go out unless it was completely necessary, many car insurance companies started offering discounts to their customers since most people were not driving very much. At about the same time, the federal government decided to give every adult a $1,200 check, increase the amount people could receive on unemployment, and offer forgivable loans to small businesses to help out because of the loss of income many people had incurred.

The people who fared the best during this time were the people who consistently spend less than they make. There were people who took the government check and paid down a credit card to decrease the amount of their bills each month; they took the discount from the insurance company and saved that amount. Some people canceled their cable or Netflix subscription or tightened their belts in some other way like skipping the designer coffee drinks from the "green lady" and making their drinks at home. Did you know you can purchase the syrup bottles from Starbucks or the grocery store for a little more than the cost of a single drink? I even know of people who took their $1,200 check or extra unemployment money and invested it for their future.

Miranda, the journalist, like many others, had her school loans deferred at the beginning of the pandemic and also benefited from no new interest accruing. Rather than skipping the payments like many others did, she decided to maximize her payments because she still had her job and didn't need the extra money. She continued paying her monthly payment knowing that the entire amount was going to the principle since no new interest was being charged. Because of this, her loans are going away much faster than they would have. While others will come out of this still owing the exact same amount they did at the beginning of all this, she will be more than a year ahead on her payments and very close to eliminating her student loan debt entirely.

When given the opportunity to skip a payment or payments, take advantage of the offer only if you absolutely can't afford to make those payments. If you skip the payments, many times you will incur extra interest that will actually cost you more in the long run. Many mortgage companies were deferring payments for a few months for customers who needed it, but the downside was that many lenders were going to require a full repayment of those skipped months when the time period was over. Make sure you read all the fine print before accepting deals like this.

Monika decided to park two of her family's four cars and cancel the insurance on those cars until things opened back up. Even with four drivers in their household, since she and her husband were working from home and her two sons were doing remote college and remote high school, the cars were hardly ever being used. So the cars that didn't have a loan on them were parked and their insurance temporarily removed. This saved them a few hundred dollars per month. She also cancelled her house cleaner since this was a luxury and a time saver and she now had the extra time to do it herself.

There are others who didn't fare as well. They took the check and went out and bought a new television or other extravagant items. There were a few businesses that took the PPP loans and purchased new personal vehicles. When those loans come due, they will have to show how that money was spent and their loans will not be forgivable. They will have to make monthly payments for years to pay them back.

Here is the kind of thing that you can start today, before the next pandemic or other financially devastating event happens to you: create a budget or spending plan and see what you are earning versus spending. Make a plan and pay yourself first in some sort of savings account or investment, and make it automatically come out of your bank checking account. That way, you don't even have to think about it.

If there are wasteful things in your spending, you might even evaluate those and consider removing some. Robert Kiyosaki wrote in *Rich Dad Poor Dad*, "It's not how much money you make, but how much money you keep, how hard it works for you, and how many generations you keep it for." Having even a few months of expenses in a savings account could mean the difference between keeping your house or ending up homeless.

Monika had a customer who was a travel agent, and since travel was completely shut down, she didn't need Monika's help with her social media. Since she had a lot more time, she could handle it herself. This is a smart way to look at all your expenses. If you have more time and the reason you hired out this task was to save you time, it might be better for now to take this task back and save the money.

John had this to say about saving: "Save for a rainy day. We have not been hit with anything like the Great Depression. We had a few recessions but nothing like this. I hope people remember this and learn from it. When this all started, we did go out and buy about three or four months of nonperishables. We didn't prepare in all areas; I only have five gallons of water. I did stock up on ammunition. I bought 1,000 rounds of 9mm just in case. It was about $250; that same 1,000 rounds today costs about $1,000. I also have an envelope of cash in the house. I lived in New York during 9/11, so some of this was learned from that. So, save for a rainy day—it is money, personal resources, household resources. I would rather plan than not plan. Be prepared." You can follow John's advice by checking out any really good sales on nonperishable groceries and stocking up, then saving the difference over time.

Lynn told me she doesn't have a lot of personal bills. "The only debt I have is a car payment. In my personal life, I have always been responsible like that. As a business owner, I believe when you make it, don't spend it. I am not a big spender; it may look like that because I do wear nice clothes, but I get everything on sale. I have a lot saved. I think, for a business-person, I think that is very important. Just don't blow it. Don't go buy two Jaguars, you know. I don't live very extravagantly; if I did, I probably wouldn't have made it through the pandemic. Don't live outside your means. I also don't have any debt on my business.

"I didn't take anything out of my business for me personally last year. I have customers who took out second mortgages on their houses to keep their businesses going, and now they are saying, 'Why did I do that?' It took away a lot of their retirement money. I grew up in a small town in Iowa, and my parents were always prepared for retirement. That was always important, and that is how I grew up. I don't think I would have done anything different because I saw it coming."

Another trend I have heard of is some people making the move to smaller towns where the cost of living is less expensive. They are working remotely and won't be going back to the office, so it doesn't matter where they live. A few months ago, I saw an article from Millionacres, a Motley Fool service, that mentioned towns that will even give you an incentive to move there. Here are the three examples the article gave. I am sure there are probably others.

- Tulsa, Oklahoma, is offering up to $10,000 for up to 250 qualified remote workers to relocate there. In addition to that cash, those workers would receive a one-year membership at a coworking space.

- Savannah, Georgia, is offering up to $2,000 to qualified remote technology workers who relocate.

- Topeka, Kansas, is offering up to $10,000 to qualified remote workers who purchase a home there, or up to $5,000 for those who relocate and rent.

I know this would not work for everyone, but if it fits your situation, you could save quite a bit by doing this. Living in a smaller city also offers other benefits. The slower pace and lack of heavy traffic would be much better for your attitude. (See Rule Number 11.) In addition to the lower cost of living, auto insurance would most likely be less expensive in a smaller community.

This is a rule that almost all of us could take to heart and use to improve our situations. Everyone probably has somewhere in their spending habits where they could cut a little bit and save it, even if it's only $10 per week by skipping the designer coffee for a couple days or making lunch instead of going out. You could probably save this much just by using coupons at the grocery store. Over a year, that is $520. If you have credit card debt, using this to pay it down could get you a return of 16 percent or more on your money, whatever your credit card interest rate is. This could also decrease the amount of time needed to pay off your credit cards, allowing you more to save in the future. It may not sound like much, but it is more than you would have if you did nothing, which brings us to our next rule.

Rule Number 8 Recap

This chapter is good advice anytime, not just during a pandemic. The people who live beneath their means can easily survive difficult times for a while. This is one chapter where most of the "Business Heroes" I interviewed had a lot to say. This chapter is a good first step toward making yourself "essential" in the future.

We listed examples of how some people cut back, including stopping services that are luxuries such as Netflix or Starbucks, using stimulus checks and other unexpected windfalls to pay off bills or invest, or parking cars that are not currently in use and temporarily stopping the insurance on the cars. Some people even created budgets and reduced their spending to keep themselves afloat. We also mentioned not to accept an offer to skip a payment or payments unless you can't currently afford to pay. Those skipped payments will eventually come due, and usually all at once, which could put you in big financial trouble.

We even mentioned how some people are moving to less expensive cities to save money. There is an endless supply of ways to lower your bills and live beneath your means. Finally, I mentioned how even the simple act of paying a little extra on credit card debt each month can have very positive and long-lasting results.

If you want to create a budget, head over to my website where there is a downloadable simple budget you can customize.

DO THE WORK

How have you already used this rule in your life?

Can you add anything to this?

What idea(s) from this rule can you implement in your life?

1.

2.

3.

List your action steps to do this:

1.

2.

3.

RULE NUMBER 9

Don't just sit there; do something— the Newton's First Law of Motion Model

NEWTON'S FIRST LAW of Motion states, "A body at rest will remain at rest, and a body in motion will remain in motion unless it is acted upon by an external force." This simply means that things cannot start, stop, or change direction all by themselves. I don't mean to get all "sciencey." (Is that a word? It should be a word.) But doing nothing will not change the current situation. The French philosopher, René Descartes, said, "If you choose not to decide, you still have made a choice." There is also the quote by an unknown author that goes, "Be decisive. Right or wrong, make a decision. The road of life is paved with flat squirrels who couldn't make a decision."

During the pandemic, many people started working from home or were forced to stop working. In either situation, it is easy to become complacent and just sit there on the couch binge-watching TV. The Business Heroes I know still got up every day and got dressed and prepared for their day. If everyone else is crawling or not moving, you can easily get ahead just by walking. Remember the tortoise and the hare. But unlike the hare, you only need to compete with yourself. Do a little more today than you did yesterday.

The simple act of getting up and getting ready for their day put the Business Heroes way ahead of those who decided to just skip the day today and stay in bed. By doing something—anything—you are moving, and you are open to things that might come your way. No one can make you get moving. You must be that external force for yourself. The best thing you can do when things are uncertain is cling to something familiar like your morning routine. Get up, get dressed, start your day.

Even though many companies were closed or running on a skeleton crew, other businesses were hiring. I know a few people who got great, new jobs during the pandemic. If everyone else is in the do-nothing mode, you can get ahead just by showing up and trying a little. By staying busy, you are more likely to stay positive also, since you will not just be sitting there with your TV and your thoughts. (See Rule Number 11.)

When I first went full time in my business, there were days when I would wake up and have absolutely nothing scheduled.

That can be a scary feeling when this is your only livelihood. Rather than sleeping in and coasting, I would still get up, get dressed, and start my day. To keep my business moving forward, I created a spreadsheet I called "Seeds." It was based on the quote from Robert Louis Stevenson, "Don't judge each day by the harvest you reap but by the seeds that you plant." On this spreadsheet, I listed the days of the month down the side and a number of ways I could "plant seeds" for my business across the bottom. It included things like attending a networking event, sending out a letter of follow up from a networking event, posting something on Facebook, learning, giving out a business card, and many other things that I could do to move my business forward. I actually had a list from an article I had read that listed ten things to help move your business forward. I kept it on a sticky note on my computer for quick reference. If I didn't have a customer scheduled, I would spend my time planting seeds, and I would document the specific tasks I had done on this spreadsheet. If something "grew" from one of those "seeds," I would highlight that cell in yellow. This was a visual way to see at a glance what I had reaped from the seeds I planted. To keep myself motivated to continue, I even had a cover page in this spreadsheet that would recap my "seeds" for the entire year so I could see my progress. I have not used this method in many years now, because I am almost always very busy, but this could be a great tool to get you moving if you don't know where to start.

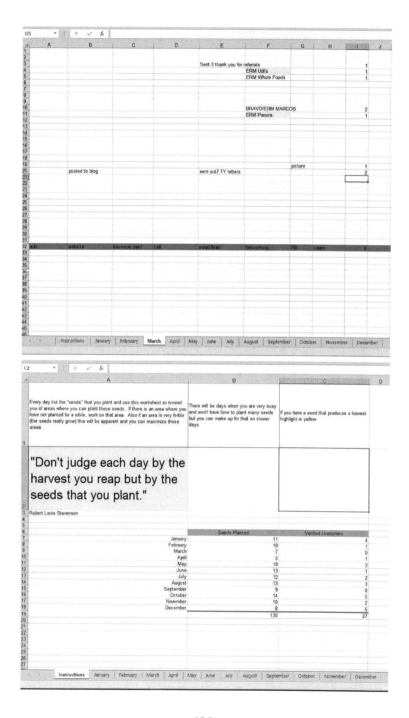

Saint Francis of Assisi had this to say about doing something: "Start by doing what's necessary; then do what's possible; and suddenly you are doing the impossible." Walt Disney talked about getting started: "The way to get started is to quit talking and begin doing." Author Neal Shusterman said, "Wailing that the sky is falling does nothing to stop it." And finally, Master Yoda said, "Do or do not. There is no try." (You read that last one in his voice, didn't you?)

Business broker Gary said, "I saw some people who went and hid in the corner, or were on the fence—didn't know what to do. You have to jump into the game. Many of my competitors went and hid in the corner, and my company is having the best year ever. We were a resource early and gave tons of free advice. I first started off as being a resource. What can I give? How can I help? Providing information as soon as it was available for small businesses. Supporting small businesses. I was persistent and consistent. I never stopped marketing. I never stopped doing my normal routine other than I normally meet people in coffee shops. That is my secret sauce: being in front of people. It has been a challenge on Zoom, but I have managed it. But it is not as good as being in person. I have stayed really busy through this whole time."

Your life can be much better in the future if you make even tiny improvements today and stick with them every day. That is the basic premise behind the popular book *The Compound Effect*, by Darren Hardy. In this book, he talks about making some small changes and doing them daily so they become new habits. Over the course of time, those small changes will add up to big differences in your life. He talks about three coworkers. One stayed basically the same. One made very small positive changes: eating healthier, getting a little exercise, and reading instead of watching so much television, and getting a good night's sleep. The last coworker made very small negative changes: not eating healthy, staying up too late watching television, and being a couch potato. After a few months, there wasn't much difference between the three, but after about a year, the differences were beginning to be highly visible.

Maybe if you are at home and just sitting around, you can get up and go for a walk. If you did this one thing every day, you would become healthier and possibly lose some weight. That would also give you more energy, which might help you in your work or your search for work. It will also improve your attitude. (See Rule Number 11.)

How about making one extra sales call per day? If you did this, over the course of a month you would make around twenty-two extra sales calls; over the year you would make about 260 extra sales calls. How would that impact your life, all from just adding one more call per day? Everyone can apply this idea to their situation. I am talking about only a very small positive change consistently carried out.

Here is what Charity had to say about doing something: "Overall, I just didn't want to not have my business anymore. I have a pretty new business; I have only been in business for three-and-a-half years. I have never made a ton of money off of it. I was starting to make really good money in February when everything crashed. I was thinking that I was finally hitting the top of the hill where I had made it. Then the pandemic hit, and everything fell off a cliff. What it comes down to is, what I do is my passion. What we do is meals for people with autoimmune diseases and chronic illness. So, we work with a lot of people who just don't feel very good on a daily basis. Changing the food you eat can really improve your quality of life. I just didn't want to give up on that. It is what I want to do. I have celiac, so I can't work in regular kitchens. I have tried, and it made me really sick. So, if I gave up on this, what was I going to be able to do? I was really motivated to just keep trying." Because Charity kept moving and trying different things, her business is currently better and stronger than it was before this pandemic even started.

A Chinese proverb says, "The journey of a thousand miles begins with a single step." Before you take that first step, you have gone nowhere. Once you start, you are on your way. The more steps you take, the easier it gets. When I started writing this book, it seemed like an impossible task, but here I am in my ninth chapter. Once I decided to start writing, the words started to come. Doing something made it happen, and it gets easier each day to continue. I set a daily goal for the number of words and didn't stop until I reached that number. Remember the proverb that basically says, "The only way to eat an elephant is one bite at a time."

Earlier in this chapter, I said that you have to be that force for yourself to get moving. While that is true, in the next chapter I talk about how you can get some help with that. You will still have to start by doing something, though.

Rule Number 9 Recap

This chapter can be summed up as taking personal responsibility. It is up to you to do the things you need to do to get ahead, to stay essential, to land that new job, and to make your life better. Another big takeaway from this chapter is to make a decision. Many times, doing these two things will put you out in front. We also talked about how just getting started will help your attitude, which can also improve your results.

I told you about my program, "Seeds," which I used to keep myself moving when I started my business. Just the simple act of doing this one thing kept my business moving forward on the days when nothing was really happening. It really is motivating to be able to look back and see what results can come from your small actions. I showed you a couple pictures of this spreadsheet, and I have included a downloadable link to this excel sheet on my website (www.BusinessHeroesofthePandemic. com) that you can customize.

I gave examples of how some of the Business Heroes of the Pandemic kept themselves moving and how this helped them see more success. Gary even mentioned how some of his competitors didn't keep moving and they suffered while he had a fantastic year.

I gave some ideas from Darren Hardy's book *The Compound Effect,* and how a few simple additions to your day can pay off big in the future.

DO THE WORK

How have you already used this rule in your life?

Can you add anything to this?

What idea(s) from this rule can you implement in your life?

1.

2.

3.

List your action steps to do this:

1.

2.

3.

RULE NUMBER 10

Don't be afraid to ask for help— the No Man is an Island Model

ACCORDING TO JOHN DONNE'S Devotions (1624): "No man is an Island, entire of itself; every man is a piece of the Continent, a part of the main."

Even if you do all the right things and make the best choices, you can still find yourself on the outside looking in. There is no shame in asking for help. I know many successful business owners, including myself, who applied for and received some of the government assistance during the pandemic. We realized that our businesses could be in financial trouble if we had a large drop in income and still had to pay the payroll and other expenses. By taking the assistance, we kept the doors open and kept employees working, since they were still getting paid also. There is truly no shame in asking for help when necessary.

Asking for help is not just about finances. If you have things going on in your business or life and you don't know how to move forward, joining a group of like-minded people, finding a trusted mentor, or even seeking professional help through a therapist or clergy could help you get past that hurdle. When times get uncertain, it is more important than ever to seek out others who might be in similar situations or those who can help you with the situations.

This is how Lynn weathered the pandemic at her business: "I'm regulated, so that makes it more difficult. I was closed down for seven weeks, then I was at 25 percent, and we just went up to 50 percent. And with the social distancing, I know I could be doing better if it wasn't the pandemic. But I am doing okay because I have five of us who are long-term employees. So, they were more comfortable with things. If I had a bunch of young, new employees, I probably wouldn't have made it. I quit paying myself and went on unemployment a few months ago. That way, I am able to pay all of my people still. They have worked for me for a long time, and I feel it is my responsibility to take care of them."

As I mentioned before, I belong to a few business groups whose members meet regularly to help each other grow and exchange referrals back and forth. Since the pandemic, we have been meeting over Zoom, and we spend a lot of this time supporting each other with ideas on how we are coping and even thriving during these difficult times. I have seen several of my colleagues in these groups reach out to others because they had an idea to help the other member's business. We also take time to review things we are trying to implement in our businesses and ask for help from the other members on how to do it. We act much like a board of directors for each other. There are many groups around like this. Meetup.com, Facebook, and LinkedIn are great places to find groups. If you can't find one, start one.

My friend, Wes, owns a drive-through coffee shop called Coffee Cabin. Since his business doesn't have inside seating, he has been mostly unaffected by the pandemic and never had to shut down. He has been checking on other businesses, and when he finds one that is struggling, he sets up a day to help it. He advertises to all his customers and also on Facebook that this business is struggling and needs some help. He then invites this business to set up in his parking lot on the assigned day and sell to his customers. He heard about a restaurant that was struggling, and it made great pies. He got a few other restaurants to help make a ton of pies, and his customers bought all the pies that day. When I went to buy my pie, I had to wait in a very long line down the street because there were so many people who came out. The local police had to direct traffic. This helped the restaurant survive when it was close to shutting its doors. It gave the restaurant a much-needed jump-start. Months later, this company is doing much better.

Wes did a similar thing for a flag company. Everyone who drove through to get coffee also purchased flags or kites.

During my writing, he has stepped up once again, this time for a local donut shop. He opened up on a Sunday (he is normally closed on Sundays) and all proceeds went to the donut shop. He also allowed the donut shop owner to sell donuts in the parking lot, and since he has advertised this on Facebook, all his customers pledged to buy a dozen or more on that day. He believes, like I do, that it is better to give a hand up, which helps foster independence, rather than a handout, which fosters dependence.

There are also a few groups I have seen on Facebook in my area that have done the same thing for businesses that were struggling. This really helps out the struggling businesses, but it also reminds everyone about the people who set up this event and, in turn, helps their businesses.

Many successful businesses owners (Business Heroes of the Pandemic) have business coaches. Just like top athletes, they want to do their best and perform like winners. This is something they started before the pandemic, and their coaches helped them weather this storm. No one knows everything, and many times you are too close to your business or situation to see where improvements can be made. Having a coach to help you stay focused is a great idea. A good coach will help you make many times what their fee is.

BK, the mortgage broker, told me, "At the beginning of the pandemic, I already had a coach." Every two weeks, he met with his coach. He had accountability to his coach, and he had accountability to his wife to make sure the coaching was effective since it wasn't cheap. His coach gave him a lot of tools and tips. One of the tools is mindset: "I would tell myself before I went to sleep, *You are going to wake up, you're going to do your devotions, you're going to make your wife some coffee, and then you are going to hit the phone. That is what you are going to do.*

"And I would tell myself that as I was going to sleep, so that when I woke up, I already had that mentality going forward. I don't check my email; I don't pull up my bitcoin balance. I don't do any of that stuff." He consistently completes his calls and finishes his day and still has plenty of time to spend with his family. He feels good because he is doing the actions needed to sustain himself going forward. (See Rule Number 9.)

Another tool the business coach gave him was to use a timer so he would stay productive and stay on schedule while on the phone. He didn't have time to chat. The call was work-related, and he could see the time ticking away, which kept him on task.

Charity also has a coach: "I have a business coach and I talked to my friends and some of the people in my coaching meetings about the things I was going through, and my business coach was so helpful. A lot of the time, I felt like I was getting knocked down and she would help me get back up and try again. I would get knocked down, and I would be down for about three or four days, and then I would come back and say, 'Okay, I am going to figure this out.'"

You can add accountability to your life and business even if you can't afford a coach. While I have been writing this book, I have made sure to tell everyone I talk to that I am writing it. This is my personal form of accountability. Since everyone knows I am writing my book, I have to complete it because I told everyone I would, and my friends and acquaintances keep asking me about it.

I lied; I didn't actually tell everyone. I told only the people who I knew would support me and cheer me on. I didn't tell people if I felt they would create a drag on my emotions and might tell me I couldn't do this. (See Rule Number 11.) This is a very important distinction. Don't let anyone crush your dreams and goals! Many of the people I told made me more motivated.

Maybe you don't want to tell everyone what you are doing, but you could tell a close friend or associate and ask that person to help keep you on top of your project or whatever it is. You can both hold each other accountable. This is a classic way to keep yourself on track and help a friend at the same time. Just like it says in Proverbs 27:17, "As iron sharpens iron, so one person sharpens another."

If you belong to a national organization, make sure you are checking in to see how others in the organization are doing.

(See Rule Number 6.) Members of Nina's organization worked together to solve their lack of in-person wine tastings. "As other people in the organization started figuring it out, everyone was asking, 'How did you do it? What are you doing?' There was a lot of idea sharing, and the company put together many training sessions to share what anyone was having success with."

Another great way to help yourself and others is through collaboration. Nina mentioned to me that she is currently collaborating with other businesses to offer more value to her customers. She has a friend who has a crafting business, and they are working together to create events around doing crafts (maybe something using wine corks) and wine tasting. (See Rule Number 7.)

BK is also using collaboration. He has partnered with a realtor, insurance agent, and accountant. They put on new home buyer seminars to help first-time home buyers navigate the many steps needed to purchase their first home. Each member of this collaboration takes a few minutes, and they share their part of the transaction. They chip in to pay for any expenses incurred for these seminars.

You could call this synergy. Together, they can draw a much bigger crowd, and because of that, they all will be more successful than they would be without the collaboration. The attendees also will get much more value from these seminars than they would if they talked to only a single person about buying a home.

Another part of "no man is an island" is helping out others when you can. Many times, I have seen business owners and friends of business owners post on Facebook about how to help out your business owner friends for no cost. You would be amazed how much these things really do help out. Here is how you can help small businesses.

If they have a Facebook business page, like their page so you will see their posts in the future. When they do make a post, engage with the post by commenting, liking, and sharing the post so all your friends will also see the post. This costs you nothing but could mean a new customer or even customers for this business. If you see someone looking for a service or product, recommend your friend's business and provide a link. You can also add how professional they are or something else about their business that might help them acquire this potential customer. I have gained many new customers due to my friends and other customers doing just this. It really helps out!

If you go out to eat at a restaurant, check in on Facebook and talk about its great food and service. You can even post a picture of the food. This puts the restaurant on others' minds, and they might end up visiting the restaurant. The same goes for small retail stores. I stop at Coffee Cabin a few times per week, and I try to check in on Facebook from there as often as I can. I often get asked by my friends about this place, and it gives me the opportunity to tell them how great it is.

The majority of this book has been about helping yourself, but it is more fun if you can go on this journey with others. Plus, this can help make sure that your favorite places will continue to survive and continue to be your favorite places.

Rule Number 10 Recap

This rule is all about community. You can't do it all by yourself, and even if you could, wouldn't it be better if you had others along for the trip? We looked at both sides of this.

There is no shame in asking for help when you need it, and it is foolish not to. You need to find a team to help each other out with advice, a leg up, and even emotional support if necessary. If there are things going on that you can't handle, you should seek out a therapist or clergy member to help you with those issues.

If you own a business, you should consider a business coach, or at least a board of directors to help you with those tough decisions and close calls. This can also help you with accountability to keep you on track with your goals. If you don't belong to a group like this, join one or start one.

We mentioned a great business idea, which is collaboration. If you can find a way to use this in your business, you will be in a much better spot and you will be able to offer more to your customers.

Finally, we gave you ways to help your friends' businesses or just your favorite businesses. These things cost you nothing but can make a big difference to the businesses you help. If you own a business, I am sure the businesses that you help in this way will reciprocate and post for you too.

DO THE WORK

How have you already used this rule in your life?

Can you add anything to this?

What idea(s) from this rule can you implement in your life?

1.

2.

3.

List your action steps to do this:

1.

2.

3.

RULE NUMBER 11

Stay positive—
the Pronoia Model

I RECENTLY READ ABOUT a condition called "pronoia." It is a lot less known than its opposite counterpart, paranoia. It refers to people who believe, without evidence, that the world around them is conspiring to do them good or otherwise secretly help them. Wow, what a wonderful way to live! We could all use some of that. I realize that a large dose of pronoia can also lead to trouble if you walk around with "rose-colored glasses" on all the time, but I do see a hint of this in the Business Heroes I spoke to. They all share a positive mental attitude.

One of my all-time favorite books is *The Magic of Thinking Big* by David J. Schwartz. I first read it many years ago when I was involved with Amway. I have read it many times and have also given away countless copies. In it, Schwartz talks a lot about "head trash" (the negative things we tell ourselves about ourselves). We all have it and need to watch that it doesn't control us. Some of the "big" ideas in his book are "Believe you can succeed, and you will," "Think success; don't think failure," and "You are what you think you are." If you have never read this book, I highly recommend it.

It is true that your mind believes everything you tell it, so speak kindly to yourself about yourself. The people who fared well during the pandemic are the people who woke up every day and gave themselves a pep talk and also gave themselves a break if they did screw up. These same people also surrounded themselves with like-minded people. They found people who would build them up and not tear them down. (See Rule Number 10.)

Believing you can do something is usually more than half the battle. You probably have heard the quote by Henry Ford that says, "Whether you think you can, or you think you can't–you're right." I have been telling my kids this forever. Many times, when people give up, they are remarkably close to being successful. If they had only held on a little bit longer.

Remember the poem by John Greenleaf Whittier:

Don't Quit

When things go wrong as they sometimes will,
When the road you're trudging seems all up hill,
When the funds are low and the debts are high
And you want to smile, but you have to sigh,
When care is pressing you down a bit,
Rest if you must, but don't you quit.

Life is strange with its twists and turns
As every one of us sometimes learns
And many a failure comes about
When he might have won had he stuck it out;
Don't give up though the pace seems slow—
You may succeed with another blow.

Success is failure turned inside out—
The silver tint of the clouds of doubt,
And you never can tell just how close you are,
It may be near when it seems so far;
So stick to the fight when you're hardest hit—
It's when things seem worst that you must not quit.

I am sure most of us have heard this poem before, but the idea it conveys needs repeating. You never know what holding on a little longer will do for your situation.

Nina had a story about not quitting. "Be open-minded to just about anything. When this first happened, I was like,

'I don't even know how I am going to be able to do business.' When they started talking about doing things virtually, I thought, 'That cannot work.' So, I was talking to a network friend of mine, and I was telling her I was really depressed. 'I just can't wrap my head around how I am going to sell my product without people trying it first.' She called me back and said, 'That is not true. That is you holding yourself back, because people go to the liquor store every day and buy wine without trying it first. You have to get that out of your own head.' As soon as I got that out of my head, realized that I am a try-it-before-you-buy-it, but I don't have to be. It is about being open-minded and being innovative. If you want your business to keep going, you have to innovate with the market.

"If you want your business to thrive and survive, not only do you have to be innovative, but you also can't give up. If it means that much to you, you have to put your thinking cap on. You have to stop and reflect, and regroup and think, 'How can I take this in a different direction and how can I keep it going?'"

We all face hardships and difficult times. The important thing is to keep things in perspective and not just give up. Try to find something that helps you keep moving forward. When I am faced with something and I can't figure out how to get past it, I do a killer sudoku puzzle. These puzzles make me concentrate on something else and think in different ways, and usually the answer will come.

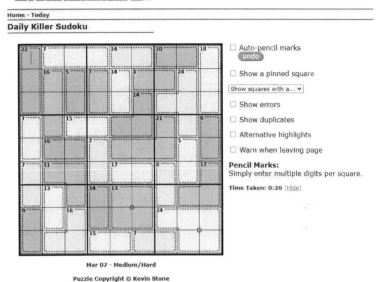

Mar 07 - Medium/Hard

Puzzle Copyright © Kevin Stone

A friend of mine told me about two people who she had spoken with on the same day. They were both in the same industry (photography) and of a similar age. When she asked how things were going, one told her of all the doom and gloom that had been happening to her. She basically said, "I can't do my business now, so I just give up." The other person told her how she had figured out a different way to do her business (she was taking people's pictures through their windows) and her customers loved the creativity, and it was thriving, and she was expanding what she does. When all else was the same, attitude and finding a new way to do it (see Rule Number 7) made the biggest difference between these two people. Remember Epictetus, the Greek stoic philosopher, from my introduction, who said, "It's not what happens to you, but how you react to it that matters."

Many years ago, I heard a story about two men sitting outside a city wall. A man came up to them and asked, "What is it like in your city?" One of the men asked in return, "Well, what was it like in the city you came from?" The traveler responded, "It was a horrible place, everyone was mean to me, and I couldn't wait to get away from that place." The man at the wall responded, "Well, you will probably find the same here." So, the traveler sadly moved on. After a while, another traveler approached the two men and asked the same question. The first man responded the same as before, saying "Well, what was it like in the city you came from?" The traveler responded, "It was a great city, everyone was so nice, and I didn't want to leave but I had to." The man at the wall responded, "Well, you will probably find the same here." This traveler was very happy and entered the city. The second man near the wall asked the first man, "Why did you tell those men two entirely different things?" The first man responded, "I told both of them the exact same thing, that they would probably find the same here. It is the same city, but their attitudes will make it a great place or a miserable place. It is up to them."

There are many tools available to help you stay positive. Some people read self-help books to stay positive, and some listen to uplifting speeches or TED Talks. Audible.com is a great place to find books and podcasts. You can listen to them while you are commuting, so it actually saves you time and makes you more productive. Some people have positive attitude posters in their offices or get positive affirmations in their email daily. Whatever works for you, find something, and stay positive.

I do a daily devotional every morning and read books to stay positive. I always have a book on business, self-help, a biography, or positive attitude available. In the last year, I have read more than a dozen books. I keep a list on my computer of books to read. (Whenever someone mentions a book, I do some research, and if I like it, I add it to my list.) When I am almost finished with one, I order another one. I find it keeps me grounded and also keeps the ideas flowing so my business can stay relevant. If I get very busy and I don't read for a few days, I can definitely feel the difference in my attitude. You can probably tell from this book that I like to have motivational quotes around to help keep me positive as well.

This is how personal chef Charity stays positive, "I think self-care is a thing that a lot of people really ignore. I have to do things like go on a run at least three times a week. I do yoga, and I eat healthy. It is little things like drinking enough water and just taking care of yourself. If I feel too overwhelmed, I go for a drive in the mountains or sometimes I go hiking. I will journal. I read daily devotionals. I read *Untamed* and some other books. I feel personal growth is very important—also trying to keep yourself in a good headspace. A lot of that is learning what it takes for you to stay there. I spent a lot of years and a lot of therapy learning what that is and doing it."

On staying positive, Lynn had this to say: "I was in a networking group with a number of women, and they were talking about manifesting, and I asked them, 'What are you guys talking about?' They said that they knew enough about me that that is just who I am. They said, 'You are a manifester; you were born with that.' I don't know if that is just my personality, or I just know how to pick myself up. Maybe I am more that way because I have employees, so I pick them up. So, it is just a habit or a mindset, because you do that your whole life for like twenty years all the time. That doesn't mean I don't get down. I was in a slump this summer; I wasn't making to-do lists. I didn't feel like it. So, I get it when people feel that way.

"Having employees who trust me and believe in me: I started to fall a little in the fall, and I could see my team relying on me and I needed to stay positive to get them up and keep things going. I also got a lot of support from long-term customers, so that really helped and made me stay positive since they all said that I was. I don't have a choice; my only choices are to close or keep going, and my long-term customers and employees make me want to continue. I didn't even have a to-do list until, like, November or December. And now, starting January, I'm just on it. I have my list, and everything is done every day. So, making a list and just sticking to it and making myself do it, and now it is just a habit again. A mindset of doing it." This is similar to the advice from Darren Hardy's book *The Compound Effect*.

It is also okay to ask some of your best customers to build you up by giving you a video testimonial or written testimonial you can share on your website, Google My Business page, or in a video on Facebook. It doesn't have to be fancy or even highly professional. Just use your cell phone to make the video. You can also ask them to place a review on your Facebook business page, your website, and your Google My Business page. By doing this, it is almost like the world is conspiring for your good. If you don't believe in yourself, how can you expect someone else to believe in you?

Rule Number 11 Recap

This rule really doesn't offer any steps to take that will move you forward and make you "essential" in the future. But this rule will help make any of the other steps you take more likely to succeed since you will have the correct mindset to accomplish the steps. The idea of pronoia is a foreign concept to many people, but it can be learned and reinforced through a steady diet of positive influence.

I mentioned a number of books, quotes, poems, podcasts, TED Talks, and other positive ideas in this chapter. I gave examples of how your attitude truly can change the outcome of your business or your life.

DO THE WORK

How have you already used this rule in your life?

Can you add anything to this?

What idea(s) from this rule can you implement in your life?

1.

2.

3.

List your action steps to do this:

1.

2.

3.

OTHER LESSONS

MY CONTRIBUTORS (Business Heroes of the Pandemic), had other great ideas that didn't necessarily fit into any of my categories (rules), so I decided to list them all here. These are also great ideas. Think hard about these and expand any that fit into your life and situation.

BK

Be prepared with systems and processes. "When the rates started dropping and the refi [refinance] boom hit, it hit fast, and it hit hard, just like the pandemic did." It took him a few months to get in a rhythm where, when someone called him, he had a process. "Okay, when somebody calls me, I do this, and then I do this, and then I do this, and then I hand it off. Okay the next one, I do this, and then this, and then that."

Gary

The guys who were successful in my business had inventory. They had businesses to sell. So always have enough inventory to weather a storm.

Stay positive. Plant your seeds. Keep connected with people, because open conversations are probably your best friend. Give when you can, whether it is your emotional support they need or even your expertise, and at that point they can't pay for it, but you have the time or you are able to give. People will remember that.

John

Expect the unexpected. Stay focused; stick with what you know.

Charity

Keep pivoting until you find the right mix.

Nina

I set boundaries; I really want to get paid for my time. I set goals with my hosts, so we both know what is expected. I don't do tastings on Friday and Saturday nights anymore. If you want my time, I am available in the afternoons, but I am going to be home with my family on those nights. I have had zero pushback on that.

Nina

This too shall pass. A good friend told me recently, 'Our lives change every three months whether you want it to or not.' So, if you look three months ago, six months ago, nine months ago, a year ago, you can see all the evolutions that have happened.

Gary and Suzanne

Keep your sales funnel full.

Marisa

Consistency and focus: I have to release a podcast episode every week and conduct interviews ongoing. I also don't allow anything to distract me from my main goals. One can easily take on too much and do nothing well. I attend to the things that matter most and pick two or three areas to tackle.

CONCLUSION

THERE THEY ARE—the eleven rules I came up with to combat being "unessential" in the future. I talked about a lot of things in this book and gave many examples. I told you many positive stories. Now it is up to you to do the things needed to move yourself forward. Remember, as Master Yoda said, "Do or do not. There is no try."

As I said in the introduction, you can pull out at least an idea or two from this book and use them to improve your own situation so the next time a worldwide pandemic or a personal tragedy happens, you will be better prepared.

If you didn't take the time to fill out the questionnaires after each chapter, go back and at least think about them. They were placed there to spur you to action so you can make a difference in your life that will help you the next time you are up against something like this. Buying the book and not using all the tools in it is kind of like buying multivitamins but never actually taking them. It is the doing, not the buying, that counts.

I hope you enjoyed this book, but more important than that, I hope this book makes a difference in your life going forward. I hope you will think about these rules when you are faced with obstacles. I hope you will pass this book along to others so they can gain something also. My ultimate hope is that you never have to go through something like the COVID-19 pandemic again, but if you do, you will be better prepared and make the most of the situation, like a Business Hero!

Take back control of your life and business by applying these rules. When you have one job, or one stream of income, whomever you report to, or whoever can change your stream of income, is in complete control over your livelihood. When you add another job (side hustle) or another stream of income, you can take back some of that control. Be your own Business Hero! *We are all essential!*

As you take some of these rules to heart and begin to move forward with new ideas, remember that not everything you try will succeed. But failure isn't caused by not succeeding. It is caused by quitting. So, if one of your ideas doesn't pan out, do something else. Don't give up. That is the only way to truly fail. As most people have heard, Thomas Edison once said this about inventing the lightbulb: "I have not failed. I've just found 10,000 ways that won't work."

If one of the ideas from this book is really speaking to you, do some research and find out more about it and figure out how to implement it into your life. Remember, time will pass regardless. Why not spend that time improving your situation?

I would love to hear from you about your success with this. Please post on Facebook at @businessheroesofthepandemic.

RULES

Rule Number 1

Always be looking for ways to reinvent yourself or your business—the Back to the Drawing Board Model

Rule Number 2

Use the current time to grow—the Butterfly Model

Rule Number 3

Everybody needs a side hustle—the Don't Put All Your Eggs in One Basket Model

Rule Number 4

Look for recurring revenue—the Life Insurance Sales Model

Rule Number 5
Make money while you sleep—the Self-Service Car Wash Model

Rule Number 6
Stay on your customers' radar—the Top-of-Mind Model

Rule Number 7
Search for what isn't being done—the Outside the Box Model

Rule Number 8
Live beneath your means—the Rainy Day Model

Rule Number 9
Don't just sit there; do something—the Newton's First Law of Motion Model

Rule Number 10
Don't be afraid to ask for help—the No Man is an Island Model

Rule Number 11
Stay positive—the Pronoia Model

SUGGESTED BOOKS

Rule #1 – Always Be Looking for Ways to Reinvent Yourself or Your Business. "The Back to the Drawing Board Model."

The 4-Hour Work Week – Tim Ferriss

Rule #2 – Use the Current Time to Grow. "The Butterfly Model."

The E-Myth Revisited – Michael E. Gerber

Rule#3 – Everybody Needs a Side Hustle. "Don't Put All of Your Eggs in One Basket Model."

The Tax & Legal Playbook – Mark J. Kohler

Rule #4 – Look for Recurring Revenue. "The Life Insurance Sales Model."

Mastering Recurring Revenue – Judge Graham

Rule #5 – Make Money While You Sleep. "The Self-Service Carwash Model."

The Tax & Legal Playbook – Mark J. Kohler

Rich Dad Poor Dad – Robert Kiyosaki

Rule #6 – Stay on Your Customers' Radar. "The Top-of-Mind Model."

How to Win Friends and Influence People – Dale Carnegie

Rule #7 – Search for What isn't Being Done. "The Outside the Box Model."

Outliers – Malcom Gladwell

Mad Genius – Randy Gage

Rule #8 – Live Beneath Your Means. "The Rainy Day Model."

The Total Money Makeover – Dave Ramsey

Rule #9 – Don't Just Sit There, Do Something. "The Newton's First Law of Motion Model."

The Compound Effect – Darren Hardy

The Slight Edge – Jeff Olson

Rule #10 – Don't Be Afraid to Ask for Help. "The No Man is an Island Model."

The 7 Habits of Highly Effective People – Stephen R. Covey

Rule #11 – Stay Positive. "The Pronoia Model."

The Magic of Thinking Big – David J. Schwartz

ABOUT THE AUTHOR

DUANE MCHODGKINS is the owner and operator of Duane's Reliable Computer Services in Parker, Colorado, where he lives with Becky, his wife of thirty-six years, and Misty, their long-haired chihuahua. He has two grown children, Miranda and Parker, who gave him insight into the struggles of younger people during the pandemic.

Duane has grown his business and adapted to changing conditions for more than ten years, helping small businesses and individuals manage their technology issues. Many of the ideas for this book came from his personal experience as a successful business owner and from his friends and networking partners who also have built successful careers. Prior to running his own business, Duane worked in a management capacity in a number of other successful companies. He learned about being innovative and resourceful while serving in diverse roles in the business world.